Requirements for Greatness

Justice, Mercy & Humility

Lori Wilke

Destiny Image® Publishers, Inc.
P.O. Box 310
Shippensburg, PA 17257-0310
"We Publish the Prophets"

ISBN 1-56043-152-0

For Worldwide Distribution
Printed in the U.S.A.

Destiny Image books are available through these fine distributors outside the United States:

Christian Growth, Inc.
Jalan Kilang-Timor, Singapore 0315

Omega Distributors
Ponsonby, Auckland, New Zealand

Rhema Ministries Trading
Randburg, Rep. of South Africa

Salvation Book Centre
Petaling, Jaya, Malaysia

Successful Christian Living
Capetown, Rep. of South Africa

Vine Christian Centre
Mid Glamorgan, Wales, United Kingdom

WA Buchanan Company
Geebung, Queensland, Australia

Word Alive
Niverville, Manitoba, Canada

Inside the U.S., call toll free to order:
1-800-722-6774
Or reach us on the Internet: **http://www.reapernet.com**

Contents

Introduction

When God calls us to become great, it sounds exciting and adventurous! It captures our interest with the possibilities or opportunities that might await us. Our heart cries out and says, "Yes, Lord, use me! I want to be great in Your Kingdom." In response to our prayer God begins to show us what we've been called to do. He reveals our gifts, our abilities, our talents, and our very reason for existence. Our heart explodes with anticipation; we know we have a "divine purpose" on the earth!

Then we learn that all these gifts, abilities, and talents are useless in God's Kingdom unless we possess certain of His characteristics. Why? Those same abilities that God gave us as strengths can also be our greatest weaknesses. Our strongest gifts and talents can be our greatest opportunities for defeat. Potential is like the atom: The smallest thing in the world, when it is split, becomes the biggest. That's the way God's Kingdom is. In the Kingdom of God, the best way up is down. The best way to receive is to give. The best and only way to become great is to serve.

Jesus overheard His disciples disputing one day about who was the greatest. So He sat them all down together and said, "Look, boys, here's how things work. If anyone really wants to be number one, you need to act like you're the last. You need to go around and serve everybody else. Then you'll be the greatest. That's just the way My Kingdom works!"

Even in our serving, God's greatness depends on godly character. His promotion process is protected by godly principles. His power is guarded by problems. As we cry out to fulfill God's purpose on the earth, we must also find out, "What are the requirements for greatness?" As we pursue the position of leadership God has called us to attain, we must continually ask, "What does the Lord require of me?"

As we discuss the answer to that question throughout the pages of this book, I want us to keep in mind the awesome promises of guidance and strength that God gives us.

I will instruct thee and teach thee in the way which thou shalt go: I will guide thee with Mine eye (Psalm 32:8).

If we remain teachable and yielded before the Lord, He will fill our lives with wisdom. As we continually humble ourselves in the sight of God, He will raise us up and cause our lives to prosper. As we submit to His Word in faith and obedience, He will bring our lives to a place of greater and greater influence on this earth.

To live in a place of humble trust and teachableness before the Lord, we must only have eyes for Him. When searching for the highest and greatest symbol of devotion he could glean from his life, King Solomon penned the Song of Songs, or Song of Solomon, to his beloved Shulamite bride. Under the inspiration of God, the wisest man chose a symbol that perfectly describes the ideal state of the Church, the Bride of Christ. This symbol describes what God longs to see in you and me:

vi

*Behold, thou art fair, my love; behold, thou art fair; **thou hast doves' eyes*** (Song of Solomon 1:15).

What is so significant about doves' eyes? When I began to seek the Lord and do research, I discovered that the eyes of a dove are different from those of other animals, and from those of people. The dove can only look in one direction at a time. It has "single vision."

The most ancient and unchanged command that God has given to man is, "...Thou shalt love the Lord thy God with all thy heart, and with all thy soul, and with all thy strength, and with all thy mind; and thy neighbor as thyself" (Lk. 10:27).

This command is at the core of what will be seen in real greatness: loving God and loving people.

God is bringing the Church back to the real definition of greatness by revealing "the weightier matters" of His Kingdom. It is easy to become distracted by the urgent things in life and ministry while neglecting what is most important to God.

What does God consider important? People are important to God—hurting, broken, dying, and lost people! God seeks for intercessors to stand in the gap. He calls for the workers to reach out and reap the harvest. He needs the messengers who will carry His Word to the ends of the earth. He looks for the servants who will share His love and healing with a world filled with violence and death.

Our lives will be great today if we simply do what God does and say what God says. Why? Jesus said, "My Father...is greater than all..." (Jn. 10:29). The more we become like our Father, the greater we will be.

The prophet Jeremiah told Baruch the son of Neriah, "And do you seek great things for yourself? Do not seek them..." (Jer. 45:5

NKJ). The difference between seeking "greatness" and seeking "great things" is in the word *yourself.* God desires for us to seek greatness, but not for ourselves. Our greatness is for others. If it is not for others that we seek to attain greatness, then it cannot be Kingdom greatness. God raises up great leaders to serve their followers. Followers are not raised up to serve great leaders.

Jesus spoke to the religious leaders of His day and said, "Woe unto you, scribes and Pharisees, hypocrites! for ye pay tithe of mint and anise and cummin, and have omitted *the weightier matters* of the law, *judgment, mercy, and faith*: these ought ye to have done, and not to leave the other undone" (Mt. 23:23). Self-appointed leadership gravitates toward serving itself. God-appointed leadership gravitates toward serving people and modeling godly character and influence in their lives.

Before God raises you up as a leader, you must first answer this question: "What does the Lord require of me?" As you read this book, let God encourage you and inspire you to come up a little higher in your calling as a leader. Let Him empower your life so that you might walk in the high calling of servanthood and godly character. Hear the voice of His Spirit instructing and guiding you to new levels of growth and change. Feel the passion of His heart motivating you to rise out of callous complacency to fruitful fulfillment. As leaders of His end-time Church, called to demonstrate His greatness and glory to the earth, let us be faithful not to omit "the weightier matters" of His Kingdom.

Thomas Wilke, Senior Pastor
Spirit Life Church/Hebron Ministries
Milwaukee, Wisconsin

Part I

Justice

Chapter 1

Justice Is More Than a Word

If you are out to please man, you will never walk in integrity with God.

Most of the problems you and I face on an average day are *relational*; that is, they stem from our relationships with other people. In fact, much of the suffering we endure results from our broken relationships, betrayals, and personal disappointments with people and ourselves. How do you respond to the relationships placed in your life? How do you deal with the suffering that occurs because of those relationships? I have found that the best way to deal with personal relationships is to walk in the principles of God's Word. God tells us how to respond to others:

*Woe unto you, scribes and Pharisees, hypocrites! for ye pay tithe of mint and anise and cummin, and have omitted the **weightier matters** of the law, **judgment, mercy, and faith:***

3

these ought ye to have done, and not to leave the other undone (Matthew 23:23).

God is constantly trying to get us to face these three major relational issues in life: justice (judgment), mercy, and humble faith. These are the things that really matter to Him. Jesus was saying to the Pharisees in this passage from Matthew that some things in life are just more important than others. Jesus refers to these three principles as "the weightier matters."

The Old Testament reference for Jesus' quote is found in Micah 6:8:

He hath shewed thee, O man, what is good; and what doth the Lord require of thee, but to do justly, and to love mercy, and to walk humbly with thy God?

One day several decades ago a bomb was thrown onto the porch of a man by the name of Martin Luther King, Jr. No one was hurt in the explosion, but afterward Dr. King spoke to those around him who thought that justice could be gained by violence, saying that justice could only be found by returning hatred with love.

Dr. King became the foremost leader in bringing justice to the black people. Dr. King believed that gentleness and peace were more influential than violence and hatred.

Each year new advancements came that brought greater justice and equality for the black people. The movement was non-violent, and although some demonstrations were met with violence, Dr. King and those following him refused to answer violence with violence.

In 1963 Dr. King was able to bring a quarter of a million Americans to Washington, D.C., to support justice and equal rights for everyone in America. Dr. King spoke to us on the dream that he had. (And I should add, the dream God has.) "I have a dream,"

4

he said, "that one day this nation will rise up and live out the true meaning of its creed: We hold these truths to be self-evident, that all men are created equal."

In 1964 Dr. King was awarded the Nobel Peace Prize. Although he was shot to death by an assassin on April 4, 1968, his memory and message of justice lives on forever. Martin Luther King, Jr.'s life was a living testimony to the pursuit of one of the most important, weightier matters to God: *justice.*

Greatness in the Kingdom of Light is not comprehended by the kingdom of darkness. In fact, to the darkness of men's minds and hearts, Kingdom greatness seems foolish, repulsive, and something to be avoided as an unnecessary hardship. That is why, to fully become great, we must have God's unique perspective divinely imparted to us. God must share with us not only a mental understanding of its design and substance, but also an inner or spiritual transformation so our lives can embrace it.

The Integrity of Justice

What is justice? Justice is "the quality of being just or fair." It is the principle of moral rightness and equity, of conformity to moral rightness in action or attitude. It implies making a decision or a verdict that is right, fair, innocent, and reasonable. Micah the prophet emphasized the very same things in the passage quoted earlier.

Justice is characterized by a decision to walk in integrity before God. Justice also is marked by a decision to walk in integrity before others. Jesus exposed the hypocrisy of the Pharisees (the religious leaders of His day) who were doing one thing and saying another. Our number one priority is to walk in integrity toward God, and our chief desire should be to honor Him.

The Pharisees were men-pleasers who were always "play acting." That's what being a hypocrite means. These were the masters of "religion on a stage." They wanted to look good before men, which really means they didn't care about what God thought. It is important for us to pay close attention to Jesus' warnings about the Pharisees because they were the religious establishment, the "spiritual elite" of Jesus' day. It is vital that the spiritual leadership of the Church today pay attention to the Lord's words. God said these Jewish leaders were like dead men's bones in a pretty, whitewashed burial sepulcher! In other words, they appeared to have everything in order on the outside, but inside there was nothing but corruption, deadness, and deceit. They were living a life of rules and regulations for show rather than a life of substance. They sacrificed integrity with God for the popularity of the people.

How can ye believe, which receive honour one of another, and seek not the honour that cometh from God only? (John 5:44)

God asks, "How can you even live, how can you exist when you are always looking to please the unstable opinions of men?" Just decide to walk in integrity toward God no matter what people think, no matter what happens, no matter who goes with you or who doesn't go with you. Go all the way with your God!

This is the kind of inner strength and character that will help you face the fire of difficulty and adversity in life. The fiery trials most often come in areas where you must walk on with God, even if nobody else is walking with you.

Why is justice so important to God? One reason is that justice is the exact opposite of the devil's lies and deceptions. The devil is the father of lies, an accuser and a slanderer. He is out to impress, but inwardly he is a deceiver. Once we begin to fear the disapproval of men, we begin to walk in lies and injustice because we have forsaken our integrity toward God. It makes me sad to admit that a Christian's "word of honor" is becoming obsolete and worthless in this day. We have forgotten how to live a life based on honesty and integrity. Even worse, we've backed away from what real covenant means in our relationships!

Our Word of Honor

At one time people considered their word of honor-to be so important that they would give their lives to preserve and protect it. When our words become worthless, no one cares what we say. If we think that we can do something just because of "who or what we are," we become proud and our word means nothing. When we are asked to keep our word and fulfill a commitment we make to the local church or to a brother, it is easy to say, "I don't have grace for that, or that's not my gift or personality type," or worse yet—"The Spirit of God hasn't led me in that direction." The strange thing is that we thought we could handle the responsibility when we gave our word originally. When we break such promises, our word becomes as worthless as our discernment.

The Psalmist penned a word from God that describes true covenant in the Kingdom. We need to rediscover and rededicate ourselves to faithfulness and integrity toward God and the brethren again:

Lord, who shall abide in Thy tabernacle? who shall dwell in Thy holy hill? He that walketh uprightly, and worketh righteousness, and speaketh the truth in his heart. He that backbiteth not with his tongue, nor doeth evil to his neighbour, nor taketh up a reproach against his neighbour. In whose eyes a vile person is contemned; but he honoureth them that fear the Lord. **He that sweareth to his own hurt, and changeth not.** *He that putteth not out his money to usury, nor taketh reward against the innocent. He that doeth these things shall never be moved* (Psalm 15).

In my personal life I want to have so much integrity that I will swear to my own hurt and change not. That is the mark of true covenant. That is faithfulness and integrity toward God. I don't want to lie and say, "God hasn't led me into that area," or "I no longer feel led to do that." I want to speak the truth and say, "It's hard, and it may hurt me, but I'm going to keep my word and fulfill my commitment by the grace of God."

God's people earn a sad reputation in the world when we do not walk justly before men or God. **When we do not walk in justice or integrity, it disqualifies us for greatness.** He wants us to deal with our sin and let our roots go down even deeper to where we will find the grace we need to live honorable lives.

Yes, we may still be tempted to make excuses. We may still get so tired that we want to shade the truth so we don't have to keep our word. We may even be tempted to do some religious "activities" to make ourselves look super spiritual like the Pharisees, but we need to resist that temptation to sin. Pride can lead to all kinds of deception.

God wants to *transform* and *empower* your inner man with passion and strength. He will not stop at mere transition. **God wants to totally remake your inner composition and structure to mirror His own integrity.** As we let our roots sink down deeper into the soil of God's love, we will receive His power and strength to fight the "good fight of faith" (1 Tim. 6:12).

Every day, we need to remind ourselves that it is God's grace alone that will save us, and that we are held accountable for every word.

A good man out of the good treasure of the heart bringeth forth good things: and an evil man out of the evil treasure bringeth forth evil things. But I say unto you, That every idle word that men shall speak, they shall give account thereof in the day of judgment. For by thy words thou shalt be justified, and by thy words thou shalt be condemned (Matthew 12:35-37).

Our Integrity With God

When we read and meditate on God's Word, our integrity becomes focused on the Word of the Lord and upon God Himself. If your daily life is rooted in a secure relationship with God, you will be at peace with both God and man. **The first step is to realize that God made a decision and decreed a verdict and judgment over your life—"not guilty"!** That divine decision is final, and God's justice was settled and sealed by the blood of Jesus Christ on the cross. His decision is *for* you, not against you. You have been justified, or declared just, by the blood of the Lamb! (See Romans 5:9.) Man's part of the case is to accept by faith what God has decreed because of His redemption.

God has executed justice. The Holy Judge in Heaven says, "I proclaim you freed from sin!" Now we can stand before God with His integrity with His righteousness and say, "God, because You judged me and declared me to be innocent in Your mercy, now I want to walk in integrity with You and others in the same way. I ask for Your help to extend that godly mercy and verdict of innocence toward others."

The Pharisees were insanely jealous of Jesus because He was able to influence the multitudes by the mercy, grace, and love of God. There is no room for condemnation in the heart of God. He says to all, "You may come to Me just the way you are. All are welcome at My table." The legal condemnation of man says the opposite: "Don't come to me until you meet my standards. You're not worthy of my attention or acceptance until you conform to my ideas." This produces the fear of rejection. When we give in to the fear of man, the Bible says that fear "bringeth a snare," which in turn opens the door to rejection (Prov. 29:25).

What happens when you commit yourself to walk in integrity toward God? You will discover something miraculous when you dare to declare, "God, even if nobody else goes with me, I'll stand with You and be accountable to You. Even if nobody else comes along, I'll stick with You." God describes the miracle in His Word: "Delight thyself also in the Lord; and He shall give thee the desires of thine heart" (Ps. 37:4).

Our attitude must be to relate to God with justice and integrity. I believe most people want to do that, and Christian disciples intrinsically have that desire in some form or another. Our problems usually arise when we get subtly caught up in the pharisaical fear of man. I've noticed that whenever I give my word to our daughter, Laurelle, she remembers what I say. "Well, Mom, I thought you said...." She accurately reminds me of any promises or statements I have forgotten. The Lord says we will someday account for every word we say. In practical terms, that means when you say you will be someplace at nine, then you must be there at nine! When you tell someone, "Yes, I'm going to try to help you," then you keep your word and show up to help that person—even if it is inconvenient or financially painful. Don't ever give your word of honor if you are not going to keep it.

Our Integrity With Others

Most of our problems with justice arise from the way we respond to other people around us. I have found five major guidelines in God's Word to govern our covenant relationships with others. By following these biblical principles of justice in our actions and attitudes, most if not all of our relational problems will be removed because we will respond to others with the heart of

God. Here are five questions that will guide us to a life of integrity and justice.

Five Fruits of Justice and Integrity

1. Do your actions and attitudes bring dignity and significance to others?

2. Do your actions and attitudes provide others with purpose, hope, and a powerful positive future?

3. Do your actions and attitudes bring individuality to others? Do they allow others to be creative individuals?

4. Do your actions and attitudes give others a sense of safety and protection?

5. Do your actions and attitudes cover others' mistakes, releasing them from sin through forgiveness and restoration?

Our integrity with others is one of the most important things we need to preserve. In my travels, I have noticed that people in other countries seem to have a better understanding of integrity than Americans. Most nationalities outside of America have a superior understanding of and commitment to *covenant* relationships. They understand that when you give your word, you back your word with your *entire being and action.* Sometimes we avoid keeping our word by misusing the valid concept of spiritual guidance with the hollow excuse, "I know I said it, but you see, the Spirit didn't lead me to do that today."

God is pulling us back to the bedrock of His own integrity. He is saying, "When you give your word of honor to other people, then *stand by your word*—though you swear to your own hurt, you change not!" He longs to dwell with someone who " backbiteth not with his tongue, nor doeth evil to his neighbour, nor taketh up a reproach against his

11

neighbour. In whose eyes a vile person is contemned; but he honoureth them that fear the Lord..." (Ps. 15:3-4).

This "swearing to your own hurt and changing not" applies to every covenant—especially the marriage covenant. My father is a pastor, and one day he looked me straight in my face and said, "Honey, you can marry who you want to, but you better make sure you marry him for life." He made it clear that I didn't have any options. "When you are married, you are married!" That's what my father said. I'm thankful that today I have a good husband. No one could love her husband more than I do. Together we make allowances for each other. Integrity in our marriage relationship means working to help the other fulfill God's calling as a leader and as an individual.

With all the things we go through in our marriages and close relationships, we must learn what God means when He talks about covenant. To put it bluntly, it means "swearing to your own hurt in areas of commitment and relationship and changing not."

For a time, Tom and I were called exclusively to the traveling ministry. When Tom, my husband, received a clear call of God to pastor a church, I remember looking at him and thinking, "God, I don't know if I'm prepared to handle that." I knew the commitment would require great meekness, patience, and wisdom. I just didn't know if we were prepared. I found out how humble I could become during this time. Challenges to your personal desires let you find out how much you really need to grow. When you deal with relationships, marriage, and personal covenants, your character is tested. At that point I wondered if the evangelistic ministry would continue or die. God told me, "Don't worry and fret about it. You just honor your covenant with your husband. Love him, prefer him, and put the pastoral ministry first. When you do that, when you esteem him better than yourself, I will take care of you."

This word of wisdom applies to every covenant relationship. When we esteem others better than ourselves, we can work out anything. I had traveled a lot and enjoyed it very much, so to refrain from traveling and ministering for a season was one of the hardest things I've ever done. After a season, God released me to travel a little at a time. All the while, a deeper love and commitment for those in our church was burning in my heart. I realized that God was adding responsibilities to my life, not subtracting some. Because I had been faithful with His gifts and callings, He was allowing me to be a support to my husband in pastoring people, which is the highest responsibility anyone could ever have.

God commands us to live justly and to deal justly with everyone we encounter. It is part of our calling as Christians and our commission as disciples of Jesus Christ. As witnesses of Christ and teachers of the gospel of the Kingdom to the nations, we are required to demonstrate God's nature of justice and integrity toward people. The apostle John said we were not to "love in word, neither in tongue; but in deed and in truth" (1 Jn. 3:18). That principle makes justice more than a word. Justice is an attitude, a character quality, and a spiritual force. Justice is part of the very nature of God and a "weightier matter" of God's Kingdom. Let's begin to learn how to produce the five fruits of justice in real life, where "true religion" really counts.

Chapter 2

The Five Fruits of Justice

Every living soul is significant to God, no matter how many
ways other people find to disqualify them.

If you live in California, Florida, or Arizona, you can probably
simply step out into your yard and pick your choice of oranges or
grapefruit each morning for breakfast. What can your neighbors
pick from your tree? Justice is like a fruit tree in a dry and barren
land. When it bears fruit, everyone who stops to taste its fruit is
refreshed and strengthened.

God states that we are "trees of righteousness" planted by the
Lord (Is. 61:3). He planted us by the river of life so we would
produce fruit in season (Ps. 1:3). One of the fruits of righteousness
is justice, and justice refreshes, preserves, and protects all who
enjoy its fruit—even if they are in a place where justice is rare.

Jesus Christ is the "pattern son," the ultimate measure of
perfection for everything in our lives. He is also the "author and
finisher of our faith" (Heb. 12:2). One of the most important things
Jesus did was fulfill prophecy by planting justice in the earth.

...I will raise unto David a righteous Branch, and a King shall reign and prosper, and shall execute judgment and justice in the earth (Jeremiah 23:5).

Jesus is that righteous Branch that reigns and prospers in our lives. The execution of judgment and justice means that the guilty verdict of our sin has been satisfied and done away with through His substitutionary work. Second Corinthians 5:21 says, "For He hath made Him to be sin for us, who knew no sin; that we might be made the righteousness of God in Him." As the revelation of His righteousness grows in our lives, so the fruit of justice prospers and reigns through our lives.

Jesus brought justice to the lives of real flesh-and-blood people during His ministry on earth. He was a champion of the forgotten and despised members of society. He defied the religious status quo and openly mingled with sinners, prostitutes, tax collectors, and lepers. Just before His arrest, He passed His burden for justice on to us in His "high priestly prayer" when He prayed, "As Thou hast sent Me into the world, even so have I also sent them into the world" (Jn. 17:18).

Jesus' ministry to those trapped by unfair prejudice and criticism is yours also. Jesus planted justice in the earth by hanging on a tree, the lone innocent Man who died for the guilty human race.

The Lord has destined for us to produce good fruit. He planted Himself in our hearts so people would find the sweet fruit of God's justice in our lives as they deal with us. People don't look at name tags when they walk through an orchard; they look for the fruit. Our lives can be covered with the five fragrant fruits of justice and integrity!

The Five Fruits of Justice

Let's look at five ways that justice can be ministered to others. God wants to command a blessing upon us, but God can only anoint those who purpose to walk in unity with the brethren:

Behold, how good and how pleasant it is for brethren to dwell together in unity! It is like the precious ointment upon the head, that ran down upon the beard, even Aaron's beard: that went down to the skirts of his garments; as the dew of Hermon, and as the dew that descended upon the mountains of Zion: for there the Lord commanded the blessing, even life for evermore (Psalm 133).

Once again, here are the five questions that guide you to a life of integrity in your relationships with others. Bring these fruits to others and God will command this blessing on you!

1. Do your actions and attitudes bring dignity and significance to others?

2. Do your actions and attitudes provide others with purpose, hope, and a powerful positive future?

3. Do your actions and attitudes bring individuality to others? Do they allow others to be creative individuals?

4. Do your actions and attitudes give others a sense of safety and protection?

5. Do your actions and attitudes cover others' mistakes, releasing them from sin through forgiveness and restoration?

Justice Brings Significance

1. Do your actions and attitudes bring dignity and significance to others?

Jesus worked a lot of miracles, but most of the time He transformed lives by treating people *like they mattered*! **Miracles can
and should take place in our lives too. But most of the time we
will transform lives by treating people the way God does...like
they are the most important thing in the world!**

Jesus found people who were convinced they weren't good
enough to be loved or to have value, and *He gave them a new
outlook on themselves*! Jesus—our Shepherd—is a gatherer, not a
scatterer. Instead of searching for ways to exclude people from His
flock, He constantly invited them to join His feasts and share His
food! When you think and act positively toward others and make
them feel beautiful, you demonstrate the justice of God. **Every time
you treat people with dignity and respect, you demonstrate the
true meaning of God's justice.**

Every living soul is significant to God, no matter how many
ways other people find to disqualify and dismiss them. By boldly
proclaiming the gospel and reaffirming the forgiving power of the
blood of Jesus, we *qualify* people to live with God! We have the
"mind of Christ" (1 Cor. 2:16). Now we need to act like it.

Jesus looked for people who *were trapped by unfair prejudice
and unfair judgment* and showed them *how they qualified* for
equality and favor with God. We often hurt one another through
prejudice over religious ideas, dress, appearance, skin color, eth-
nicity, or past mistakes. The Gospel of John describes the day Jesus
met a Samaritan outcast, a female adulterer from a "half-breed"
race according to the Jews of that day. Jesus broke a lot of man-
made rules to minister to that woman. Jews, especially Jewish
teachers of the law, just didn't talk to or even acknowledge the
existence of Samaritans. Jesus didn't see all that. He saw a woman
in sin in need of forgiveness and restoration. Both the woman at the
well in John 4 and the adulterous woman in John 8 were in a

predicament. Women living in that society had a hard time providing for themselves. Jesus did not excuse their sin, but He understood their dilemma and He gave them the hope of a new future.

Jesus was a friend of harlots and other sinners. He didn't judge unfairly. His love is still available today to "whosoever" will come to Him. Jesus gave everybody an opportunity to become a friend of God—no matter who they were. He offered the woman of Samaria the living water of life and set her free. That is the justice of God in operation.

Jesus searched for the lost like the shepherd of the "ninety and nine" who left the flock in the safety of the fold to search for the one lost sheep (Mt. 18:12). Whenever He found people who had lost their self-respect, He gave them a sense of their own gifting and calling.

In John 9 Jesus found a man humiliated by society—a blind beggar. Jesus proclaimed justice to the man. When everyone asked if the man or his parents had sinned, Jesus set the record straight. "...Neither hath this man sinned, nor his parents: but that the works of God should be made manifest in him" (Jn. 9:3). Jesus set the blind man free from the stench of legalistic condemnation.

Critical spirits are contrary to the justice of God. A Yiddish proverb says, "A critic is like the lady who can't dance, so she says the band can't play." Jesus recognized critical, or judgmental spirits all too well. In the sight of critical Jewish eyes, Jesus said the despised Roman centurion had more faith than anyone in Israel, putting Israeli prejudice to shame (see Mt. 8:10). He elevated the Roman soldier above the Israelites. Israelites hated Romans, especially Roman soldiers, because they held them in captivity. Jesus saw by the Spirit, not by the flesh.

19

Jesus saw a woman who was not credited for her achievement and He noticed her. The woman who anointed the Lord's head with precious ointment was ignored and rejected. Jesus, however, said what she had done would be a memorial for her forever. (See Mark 14:3-9.) "For God is not unrighteous to forget your work and labour of love, which ye have shewed toward His name, in that ye have ministered to the saints, and do minister" (Heb. 6:10).

In another situation the justice of God worked in a peculiar way. In Matthew 15:22 a woman came to Jesus because her daughter was grievously harassed by a devil. At first Jesus did not answer her even with a word. Provoked by the lack of response, the woman pressed in further. Jesus then proceeded to practically call her a dog. Now how could that be encouraging to the woman?

Jesus knows what is in the heart of people and what it takes to provoke them to seek and believe God. This woman could have had a very poor self-image. Perhaps, when Jesus told her to her face what she believed she was inside, it challenged the false humility or her poor self-concept. It made her boldly face her self-concept and helped her realize what was disabling her life.

She rose up with a bit of rebellion—as anyone will when he or she can't have something. This woman thought in her heart, *I will receive this blessing.* "Even the dogs get the crumbs, Lord."

Jesus knows what it takes for us to believe that He is for us and not against us. Sometimes we need to be shocked right into the blessings of God. Jesus was bold enough to speak the truth in love.

When you give people a sense of God's favor and an ability to receive the promises of God, you are walking in the character of justice. When you give people a sense that they are beautiful, noticed, and honored, you are walking like Jesus. Someone once said, "There are two different kinds of people in the world: Those who come into a room and say, "Look, I'm here!" and those who come in and say, "Ah, there you are!" A good man always seeks to make others good.

Justice Brings Hope

2. Do your actions and attitudes provide others with purpose, hope, and a powerful, positive future?

For I know the thoughts that I think toward you, saith the Lord, thoughts of peace, and not of evil, to give you an expected end [or hope in your latter end] (Jeremiah 29:11).

With God, there is a happy ending. Never forget that. Without a sense of hope, people begin to lose life. You can live three days without water and about 30 or 40 days without food, but you cannot live one day without hope! A person with no hope can see no end to his or her difficult situation! God provides people a future and a hope. Jesus is the author of all hope.

Some of you may recall an incident in the movie *Pollyanna* where she visited a cantankerous old woman named Mrs. Snow. This woman, in her own words, lived on death's doorstep every day. One day when Mrs. Snow was picking out her coffin lining, in walked Pollyanna ready to shake her out of her despondency. Pollyanna handed Mrs. Snow a pile of sewing material and asked her to make a quilt for the upcoming fair. When Mrs. Snow rejected her offer, Pollyanna responded by saying she didn't want to visit her anymore and asked her why she always thought about dying when she was living.

Provoked by Pollyanna's question, the woman grabs the material and ends up making a beautiful quilt for the fair. She finally saw a future in giving to others relative to her own situation. She ended up happy and healed because of it.

21

You see, everyone is a world-changer. **A just man empowers others to see a future and a hope for themselves.** An individual will usually become who you encourage him or her to be. "Trust men and they will be true to you, treat them greatly and they will show themselves great" (Ralph Waldo Emerson).

You can be about the business of Jesus, provoking others to a bright future and a sure hope in God. Give children a sense of destiny from the moment they are born. Instill in them a sense of purpose, destiny, and creativity. When Jesus tells us we are world-changers, our thinking changes! We begin to take on the image of God, and God gives our lives worth and meaning. That is the God-kind of justice.

A just man is sensitive to other people's needs, as well as to their need to *be needed*. We need to know what we were born for. If you don't know you are needed, you will live your life simply for physical pleasures. Jesus says, "I need you to be a part of My plan. You have been called for a purpose, for a reason." I work closely with my husband Tom as the pastor of our church. Sometimes I am strong where he is weak, and at other times he is strong where I am weak. We work with each other to fulfill our calling in marriage and ministry. That is the way relationships work best in the Body of Christ. We work with each other to prosper and grow.

Justice Brings Creativity

3. Do your actions and attitudes bring individuality to others? Do they allow others to be creative individuals?

Some people like fellowship as long as all the "fellows" are in their ship. In other words, people want to associate with those they can understand. Always remember: Your actions can either clone people or crown people.

Christians often have very narrow-minded views of other people. We like to analyze everybody else's behavior according to

22

God's dealings with us. (Sometimes the more we know as a Christian, the meaner we get. God wants us to grow in the knowledge of His grace.) Paul warned us that God's requirements for one person may be different for another; consider his comments about eating meat and observing Jewish holidays in Romans 14:14 and Colossians 2:16). Justice is reasonable because God is reasonable. James says that God's wisdom is "first pure, then peaceable, gentle, and easy to be intreated, *full of mercy* and good fruits, without partiality, and without hypocrisy" (Jas. 3:17).

One Sabbath day, Jesus had compassion on a man with a withered hand. This man was needy, depressed, lonely, frustrated, and impaired. Jesus decided to heal the man, even though it would be considered "work" and a violation of Sabbath tradition. Legalism doesn't heal on the Sabbath, but Jesus does. Legalism won't reach out and be reasonable to needy people, but people with the heart of God will! Rules are designed to benefit people, not imprison or impoverish them! **When we bring out someone's individuality and creativity, we relate to them as God sees them.** When we become unmerciful and legalistic, our words and harsh treatment can strip people of their creativity, and they can become defiled. Still, God is reasonable and patient with us. In Isaiah 1:18 the Lord says, "Come now, and let us reason together...." God takes time to sit down and talk with us. Each generation grows from glory to glory, so let's take the time to talk and listen to each other, that our differences might not separate us but rather benefit us.

Justice Brings Protection

4. Do your actions and attitudes give others a sense of safety and protection?

True religion takes care of the widows and the orphans (see Jas. 1:27). **A just man provides covering and protection for others.** The true statistics of two different orphanages reveal the importance of dealing with the fears that every individual feels, especially with the little ones. In one orphanage 95 percent of the babies survived, as opposed to the other where only 40 percent survived. The orphanages were exactly the same in every way except for one thing. The orphanage where 95 percent of the babies survived had an elderly nurse who walked around holding and affirming the little ones. The other did not.

Providing safety to others means helping people walk through their fears, lifting others up, and defending the underdogs! That's the very heart and core of the ministry of Christ. Jesus Himself used Isaiah 61 to describe His ministry: to reach out to the broken-hearted, the captive, the blind, and the bruised. **A just man not only teaches others how to be sufficient in Christ and to provide for themselves, but also takes care of their physical needs in the growing process.** Teaching others to overcome poverty is insufficient without helping provide for their physical needs here and now!

When providing safety to others, a just man will do anything to increase the trust level among relationships. You can trust someone who walks the walk and not simply talks a good talk. I believe the primary way we teach others is through example. First Peter 5:3 exhorts the teachers to be examples to the flock. This truth remains true not only for leadership, but also for anyone who disciples others. The best teacher is a life of obedience to the principles of Christ. The spirit behind your words is often more important than the words themselves.

Consistency in the way you handle your relationships also increases the trust level. If I am up one day and down the next, people will be confused as to how to relate to me—and that confusion can breed mistrust. I cannot trust someone whom I know will always react differently to the same situation. I can trust someone who, with stability, responds consistently to the ups and downs of life. Consistency gives others a sense of safety, and releases them from their fears.

Justice Brings Forgiveness

5. Do your actions and attitudes cover others' mistakes, releasing them from sin through forgiveness and restoration?

This is one of the most important questions I can ask you! Jesus remitted and removed your sin with His own blood. Are you willing to remit the sins of others in love by forgiving and releasing them? God's purpose is always to restore people. Nowhere in Scripture does the Lord give a harder word than when He deals with forgiveness and unforgiveness! He bluntly declares, "...forgive, and ye shall be forgiven" (Lk. 6:37).

A just man forgives, even if others maliciously or ignorantly hurt him. Jesus planted a gracious nature in you that is not evil, malicious, or condemning to other people. A key to forgiveness is knowing how much we have been forgiven. God continues to forgive us moment by moment, and we may not even realize it. When you forgive others, you tear down the walls between you. Forgiveness brings unity. Forgiving people are frequently asking God to forgive them for the mistakes they themselves have made.

Forgiveness is essential for our daily life. This is one area where God is hard on us. He says if we don't forgive, He won't forgive us!

I'm not a feminist in any way—but as I compare men and women, it seems to me that the hardest thing for men to do is to ask for directions. It baffles me! They could be lost in the backside of lower Texas or Minnesota and when they finally find a gas station that is inhabited, they won't ask, "Where am I, and how do I get to civilization again?" They don't even want to get out and casually hint that they need help. It must be due to that hunter instinct inside them! They just want to drive around for five hours trying to find the place on their own. "I know it's out there somewhere!" they declare. Humorously speaking, men in general find it harder to ask for two things—directions and forgiveness.

In both cases, asking for directions and asking for forgiveness deal with the touchy area of "performance." Somehow, men feel they haven't "achieved" if they have to say, "I'm sorry." It also is difficult for leaders in any position to admit to a mistake to those they lead. Women find it a little easier because, generally speaking, they are more apt to communicate their feelings. There are exceptions, of course, for I've also seen humble men who can say they are sorry very easily.

Obviously, men and women were created by God to be very different. I'm glad that's the way God made it to be! As someone said, "Men are from Mars—women are from Venus!" There is one thing that helps men, women, and children get along, though. It's the simple phrase, "I am sorry." If we could say these words more often, ministry, marriages, and families would be a lot happier.

It is essential that we learn how to cover the mistakes of others in love. "To cover" simply means "to not publicly speak of their offenses." It does *not* mean to condone or approve of sin or wrongdoing. A just man can be a very loving individual, but he flows in injustice when he begins to publicly "uncover" someone's mistakes without his or her consent. This can happen easily in the marriage setting, where spouses claim to have forgiven their mates, but somehow everyone in the family plus all their friends seem to know exactly what the spouse did! That is not justice. That isn't even forgiveness!

Real forgiveness means you forgive and *forget* the mistake to the point where you don't hold someone accountable for it,

26

two days, six months, or five years down the road! It also means you do not spout it out to everybody else either. It's buried at the foot of the cross and it's left there. Don't dig it up! All of us make mistakes, so all of us need a ready supply of forgiveness, grace, and love.

There is a divine correlation between forgiveness and correction. A forgiving person knows how to receive correction. Some people think that correction means rejection because they have a poor self-image. The sooner they learn that he who hates correction will die (see Prov. 15:10), the better it will be for them. If you can't receive correction for your own life, then don't expect others to receive correction through you for their lives. A person who is just likes to be corrected, forgiven, then released. This is the way the just handles the injustices others do against them. They forgive and release people. Remember, your success is directly related to your ability to be corrected. Don't let pride keep you from being a forgiving person.

Part II

Mercy

Chapter 3

Mercy Makes You Real

Mercy may be late in coming, but it always ends up on top.

The cry of every human heart is "to be real." Yet we sometimes emphasize the negative over the positive, the false over the true, and the evil instead of the good. We talk more about the devil than the angels of God, and nearly every day, we emphasize mistakes more than successes. Given a choice, we usually emphasize wrong more than right.

With all the disillusionment and shortcomings in our lives, God wants us to know that *mercy makes us real*. God emphasized mercy as one of the major matters of life. It was mercy that brought God's Son to earth, a little baby in Bethlehem, as a love gift to redeem fallen man. Jesus said, "Blessed are the merciful: for they shall obtain mercy" (Mt. 5:7). The world is going through a time of distress, and its desperation for celebration is growing with every year. It's especially noticeable during the Christmas season. The world is crying out for something to celebrate while it is drowning

31

in a rising flood of negativity. The world longs for something real, personal, and touchable.

The deepest longing of my heart is to know the Lord in His reality. I ask Him to show me what is truth on a day-by-day basis. One of the richest veins of truth about His nature and heart toward us that I've found is in Psalm 145:

> *Great is the Lord, and greatly to be praised; and His greatness is unsearchable. ... The Lord is gracious, and full of compassion; slow to anger, and of great mercy. The Lord is good to all: and His tender mercies are over all His works. ... The Lord upholdeth all that fall, and raiseth up all those that be bowed down. The eyes of all wait upon Thee; and Thou givest them their meat in due season. Thou openest Thine hand, and satisfiest the desire of every living thing. The Lord is righteous in all His ways, and holy in all His works. The Lord is nigh unto all them that call upon Him, to all that call upon Him in truth. He will fulfil the desire of them that fear Him: He also will hear their cry, and will save them. The Lord preserveth all them that love Him: but all the wicked will He destroy* (Psalm 145:3,8-9,14-20).

Legalism vs. Mercy

There are two ways of looking at people. We can look at them with eyes of legalism or we can look at them through the eyes of mercy. When we are legalistic, our insecurity may cause us to relate to others in a hard, almost controlling or manipulating way. A legalistic person will look at something and be afraid, but a merciful person will look at the same thing and cling to the power and righteousness of God.

The law was given to us as a guideline. **If we emphasize the law in and of itself apart from the mercy of grace, we become helpless.** Law apart from grace makes us poor, needy, and hard—mere skeletons of what we should be. Jesus came to fulfill the law, to put the flesh of true mercy on the dry skeleton of the law. God came to warm up this earth with His mercy.

The letter of the law that legalists cling to leaves you feeling hopeless, depressed, and needy. That is its purpose; it shows you your need. If your life is based on the law, then your life is based on performance. Certain strong-willed and independent people may actually fulfill some of the law, but nobody can keep the whole law. The dangerous deception of legalism is when semi-successful "law-keepers" begin to believe that the part of the law they keep is good enough—and the part they can't or won't keep doesn't matter. They missed the whole point of the law: *Nothing we do* is good enough without Jesus! Let's not become hard, needy people living by "do's and don'ts," never knowing the love and mercy of God.

Through the person of Jesus, we can know the flesh or "human side" of the God/Man who saved us. He revealed to us His gentle softness in order for us to see the impossible become possible in our lives. As I meditated on mercy, it seemed as if I could almost see God smile. The Lord said, "Mercy is My smile."

For we through the Spirit wait for the hope of righteousness by faith. For in Jesus Christ neither circumcision availeth any thing, nor uncircumcision; but faith which worketh by love (Galatians 5:5-6).

The Power of Mercy

Faith expresses its power through mercy. Would you approach a poor or needy person and start bombarding him with Bible verses, "faith confessions," and all kinds of doctrine? No, for the person couldn't handle it. The first step of God begins with mercy. He gently brings us to the point of believing on His Son. Sometimes the mercy of God has to be expressed over and over again. I'm thankful that the Lord's mercy endures forever.

If we could see how many times we fail, and how often God covers us with His mercy, we would have a lot more mercy on others when they don't fulfill the "letter" of the law. David declared, "O God the Lord, the strength of my salvation, Thou hast covered my head in the day of battle" (Ps. 140:7). In the same way today, you and I are covered in the day of battle by the blood of Jesus. This covering was His first gift and love offering to us.

Jesus came as a baby, but He grew up so He could lay down His life and shed His blood to cover us in the day of battle. That is the mercy of God in action. I once heard a testimony about a little girl and boy who had to walk two blocks every day from their home to a bus stop to go to school. Before they left each day, their parents prayed over the children, "Father, we thank You that these little children are covered with the blood of the Lamb." They found out later that a witch lived on their block between their house and the bus stop.

After this witch became a Christian, she told how she had often watched children walking by, and she would try to persuade them to come inside and talk. Whenever children actually came into her house, she would perform odd things over them, such as curses and demonic rituals. She also said there were two children who actually repelled her every time they walked by! She was forced to turn her back and walk away from the window because those little ones were covered in the day of battle. It wasn't anything they did. Their parents simply covered them with the blood of the Lamb, which frees us from the curse of the law. Faith in the mercy of God will cover us.

Does mercy saturate your thought life when you look at others? Do you feel compassion for them? The Lord Jesus had a miracle ministry because it was His nature to love and help people, not because He wanted to prove anything. The mercy of God is always reaching out to us. We should thank God for His mercy every time we make a mistake or blow it. Many people look at mercy only as a spiritual gift, and not as an attitude that all Christians intrinsically possess. Mercy is part of the character of God, and we are all partakers of His divine nature. Christ lives within us—that hope of glory.

Thanks to the Lord's work on the cross, you have that same nature living within you! True, some people are particularly gifted in the area of mercy, but the Bible doesn't exclude anyone from allowing mercy to flow through him or her! Mercy is part of the nature of God that lives within you:

> *Charity suffereth long, and is kind; charity envieth not; charity vaunteth not itself, is not puffed up, doth not behave itself unseemly, seeketh not her own, is not easily provoked, thinketh no evil; ... beareth all things, believeth all things, hopeth all things, endureth all things* (1 Corinthians 13:4-5,7).

Mercy: Love in Action

Mercy expresses itself through love. When I was about 13, I memorized and prayed this passage in First Corinthians, inserting my name every place I saw the word love. Every day I would say, "Lori endures long and is patient and kind. Lori never is envious nor boils over with jealousy...Lori bears up under everything and is ever ready to believe the best of every person." Do you know what happened? God gave me a test after I began to believe this.

My father would drive me to school every day, for he was a teacher at the high school I attended. One day, when we pulled up to a stop sign, a guy suddenly jumped out of his car and charged toward us because he didn't like the way my father was driving. (My dad didn't like slowpoke driving.) He knocked on the glass and my father rolled down the window, thinking that maybe something was wrong with his car. The man spit on him. Needless to say, my father was stunned. He just didn't know what to say.

All of a sudden those Scriptures bubbled up inside of me and seemed to flow right out of my mouth. I said, "Sir, God really loves you," and then I smiled at him. The mercy of God turned the tables on this angry man. It was his turn to be speechless. He backed away from the car and walked away, literally flabbergasted. He didn't understand mercy. Mercy disarms the enemy.

That man wasn't flabbergasted at me; he was astounded by the power of the Word of God working through mercy! Everyone who faces situations like that can respond in the power of God, but it can only happen through the power of mercy expressing itself through love!

This happened to me twice! I was riding in a cab in New York City one time not knowing any cultural protocol. I was about 25 years old and should have known better, but I'd never been in New York before. The cab driver did not speak English. I was alone, and I didn't know how much to tip him. Evidently my tip wasn't enough because when he let me off he turned around and spit on me! (Is God trying to teach me something here?) I remember looking at him and thinking, "God loves you, brother." Once again, the love of God was in action through mercy, disarming the enemy.

A person who has a sweet spirit can actually see beyond the present situation and hold onto hope for the people who offended him or her. Mercy is the only reason you can look beyond other people's shortcomings and give them the benefit of a doubt. Mercy doesn't stop hoping and believing.

Anyone who wants to flow in mercy should put his or her name in the "love chapter" and pray it on a daily basis. It works. You will find love and mercy flowing through you in ways you never dreamed because it abides within you. You have Christ living within, and you release and express them by acknowledging His presence inside you. Try it youself. Personalize your expression of

Christ's nature abiding in you. Say, "I am merciful because I am born of God." Expand your faith in God's power working in your life by allowing the Word of God to become living and active in your heart and mind. God has given us the very "spirit of love" so we can be successful in every relationship we experience.

You can operate in good discernment if you are saturated with the love and mercy of God because you see things through unselfish eyes. Selfish people think everything revolves around them. They also take things too personally, like little children. I have never met a depressed person who was thinking about other people or who was trying to reach out and bless other people with love. Self-consciousness is also just another form of selfishness. When we get beyond that, however, we become free. Merciful people don't have to control anything because they have the favor of God. Once the favor of God is realized, the Word of God becomes active in your life. The angels of God hearken unto the voice of God's Word.

Merciful people are "feeling" people who minister to the hearts of others. Mercy is kind, everlasting, and powerful. Mercy waits patiently, knowing that God is in charge. Mercy is almost childlike in contrast to attitudes that are hard, forceful, and controlling. Mercy is very tender. Mercy is not interested so much in itself as it is in what it can do for other people. I have passed through many hardships in my life, but I have always prayed that God would keep me tenderhearted. Trials tend to make you bear up and believe through. Sometimes, in order to survive, your feelings must be made subservient to your faith. Though we all may have barrelled through the trials, we need to stay tenderhearted.

We need to be childlike. We need to be humble. We need to be real. What is real? Mercy makes you real. Mercy makes you lovable. Margery Williams' *Velveteen Rabbit* tells the story of a stuffed toy befriended by a little boy. After a series of misadventures, the rabbit learns the truth about reality through the words of his wise counselor, the "skin horse," who said:

> "Real isn't how you are made. It's a thing that happens to you when a child loves you for a very long time. You become real. Generally by the time you are real, most of your hair has been rubbed off and you get very shabby."

> "I suppose you are real," said the rabbit. "The boy's uncle made me real many years ago," said the skin horse. "You see, once you are real, it lasts for always." The rabbit sighed. He thought it would be a long time before this miracle called "real" happened to him.[1]

After facing rejection and near destruction, the stuffed velveteen rabbit was finally transformed into a real rabbit. There is a deep truth embedded in this classic nursery tale. All of us cry out in our souls, "What is real?" God extended His mercy to us through Jesus and gave us life and love. His mercy leads us to repentance and makes us soft and tender. It knocks at the door of our hearts again and again, and yet again. First He gives His sacrificial love to us, then we give our love to someone else sacrificially. It is God's mercy that gives us hope that we too can become "real" and tender like Jesus.

---

1.   Margery Williams, *Velveteen Rabbit* (New York: Platt & Munk, Publishers, 1987).

Chapter 4

Put Down the Sword

Your response to a vicious assault can instantly reveal the Christian values by which you live. —James Dobson

And, behold, one of them which were with Jesus stretched out his hand, and drew his sword, and struck a servant of the high priest's, and smote off his ear. Then said Jesus unto him, Put up again thy sword into his place: for all they that take the sword shall perish with the sword (Matthew 26:51-52).

The fastest way to be disqualified for greatness and become the enemy of God is to attack what His Son died for. In our efforts to be right, defend what we believe, or even stand up for "what is ours," the swords of judgment and accusation can become powerful weapons in our arsenal of self-preservation. Trusting in God to be our defense and vindicator is something we learn as we grow in our leadership. If we take matters into our own hands we only destroy what God is building.

In our attempt to do right, be humble, serve others unselfishly, and be obedient to God's vision for our lives, we will encounter misunderstanding and even rejection from others.

Jesus demonstrated a perfect example of greatness to the world by forgiving those who acted unjustly toward Him. He was rejected, persecuted, mocked, misunderstood, and eventually put to death. He was criticized, laughed at, used, and lied about. In all of life's injustices, Jesus was greater than all the lies and mistreatment that His enemies threw at Him. Even in His last moments before death He prayed for His Father to forgive all who wronged Him (see Lk. 23:34). This was a perfect example of greatness, not because it saved Jesus' life but because it saved everyone else's life.

When betrayal came through the kiss of a friend, He resisted the temptation to let His impulsive disciple Peter defend Him. Jesus' words to Peter silenced all other thoughts or ideas of how true greatness responds to injustice when He said, "Put down your sword, Peter, for everyone who defends himself with the sword shall die by the sword" (see Mt. 26:52). Whenever Jesus spoke about greatness, He revealed that it wasn't what you did for yourself, but what you did for others that really mattered. The "weightier matters" of justice, mercy, and humility all bring home this one point: "Vengeance is Mine; I will repay, saith the Lord" (Rom. 12:19b).

Life is filled with injustices, mercilessness, and unbelief. What you do in the midst of those attacks will determine the level of greatness you obtain. Everyone experiences woundings, scars, and long days when our hearts are filled with confusion or despair. God wants to put a song of deliverance in your heart that will resurrect you from the dead to become a living letter of God's mercy and love. He has a power available through His Holy Spirit that can break through the darkness of depression into the brightness of joy and enthusiasm. Life takes on a fresh excitement and passion when you really understand God's love for you. It is a miserable day for the devil when you discover and believe that you are really a free person, no longer bound by evil powers, sin, and guilt—that you are no longer bound by the limitations of your feelings, circumstances, and the actions or words of those around you.

God's Grace Produces Greatness

Greatness is developed not from what we do, but out of who we are. It is continually being formed by the inner strength that comes from a dependence on God's grace. **Worldly greatness comes from the outside or what we do. Spiritual greatness comes from the inside or who we are.** The apostle Paul said, "But by the grace of God I am what I am" (1 Cor. 15:10a).

I know it is because of God's grace that I am a minister today. When I started to sing as a young girl, many people told me, "Your voice is nice, but it's so small." I continued to sing and practice. I developed the small amount of skill God had given me, knowing God's grace was sufficient. I was faithful to keep practicing and seeking the Lord for what He had called me to do, even though much negative influence could have discouraged me. God said, "Lori, someday I'll use those negative words to help you. You will share them with other people who are in the same position and feeling helpless. Then I will use you to encourage and strengthen them in their calling."

It hasn't been an easy road. Faithfulness to our gifts and callings never is. When everyone else wants to change us, betray us, or even crucify us, we need to put down the sword of self-defense and let God's grace prevail! God knows what He has called us to do and has promised to be faithful to perfect those things in us. Our part comes in not quitting in the face of adversity, in not reacting in the face of rejection or personal affronts. God's power becomes defensive for us. Most of the armor of God is defensive in nature. Great people are those who endure through the most hostile of situations.

Much of my life is a story of brokenness, obstacles, and setbacks. Many times I've felt unworthy and inadequate for what God called me to do. I've learned like the apostle Paul that it is only by the grace of God that I am who I am. It is only by the mercy and love of God that I can do what God has called me to do. Time and time again, I've seen His invisible hand of mercy pulling me through.

God's Mercy Sustains

God has always reached out in His love to the distressed, the wounded, and the weary. Man's pointed finger of blame brings condemnation, but God's uplifting hand of mercy brings acceptance. That mercy and grace from God's hand are always there to lift us up from the blows of rejection and condemnation. **His mercy is an absolute spiritual force empowering us to overcome every obstacle blocking our way, whether it is emotional, physical, or spiritual.** The apostle Paul told Timothy to "be strong in the grace that is in Christ Jesus" (2 Tim. 2:1). God's mercy makes us strong and bold so we can stand before one or perhaps thousands of people and share what great things God has done for us.

When we operate in the mercy and grace of God, there is no room for criticism and judgmentalism. Lowering others or even ourselves never produces greatness, only littleness. The merciful hand of God reaches out to others with compassionate acceptance. Mercy does not need to understand in order to forgive. It does not need to defend or preserve itself in order to maintain a position of power. Mercy is rarely accepted as the status quo or the Wall Street way of getting ahead. Mercy may be late in coming, but in the end, it will always end up on top!

When we look into the light of God's mercy and focus our eyes on Him, He changes our perspective. Have you ever looked into a very bright light and then turned to look at something else? All you could see was the light lingering in front of your eyes. As we look into the face of Jesus and behold the light and brightness of His love, all we will see in others is His mercy and love toward them. Paul said, "But we all, with open face beholding as in a glass the glory of the Lord, are changed into the same image from glory to glory, even as by the Spirit of the Lord" (2 Cor. 3:18).

We see an example of this with Jacob and Esau in Genesis 33. Jacob and Esau were enemies until the day that Jacob had a confrontation with God. He actually wrestled with an angel of God and prevailed. His name was then changed from Jacob, meaning "deceiver," to Israel, meaning, "prince or ruler with God" (see Gen. 32). After this change Israel reached out to his brother Esau, trying to restore the relationship. After embracing his brother, Israel said, "For therefore I have seen thy face, as though I had seen the face of God..." (Gen. 33:10b). Once Jacob had been in God's presence, beholding His face, then all he could see was God in his brother.

God's mercy endures forever and His love for you is beyond measure! In Psalm 91:14a He says, "Because he hath set his love upon Me, therefore will I deliver him." The saints and martyrs of old submitted to fire, hungry lions, and the chopping block with raised hands in worship to the Lord as they demonstrated mercy and forgiveness toward their oppressors.

Jesus is the merciful One, but He clearly warns us that we will be judged by our own words (what an awesome thought!). Jesus said, "And if any man hear My words, and believe not, I judge him not: for I came not to judge the world, but to save the world. He that rejecteth Me, and receiveth not My words, hath one that judgeth him: the word that I have spoken, the same shall judge him in the last day" (Jn. 12:47-48).

God our Father is the Judge, but here and now a heavenly ministry of mercy is being distributed to us and through us by the Lord Jesus Christ. He uses us to touch, lift up, and heal sinners who long to repent. To all who come in genuine repentance, He says to them through our lips, "Go and sin no more." He still speaks to prodigal sons and daughters through our lips, "I've been waiting for you to come home. I've been looking forward to the moment when I could wrap My arms of love around you and put My ring on your finger. Come with Me to a celebration party given just for you!"

Our heavenly Father stands before a war-weary world with outstretched arms and says, "Come unto Me, those who are weary and heavy-laden. Follow the things of My Kingdom, for they are full of mercy and grace. Learn of My ways, which are justice, mercy, and humble trust." This loving Father woos us by His Spirit to a higher dimension of life. Through our example He desires to demonstrate His greatness to this world condemned by its own self-righteousness. He wants to show them the way. He wants them to know that He is for them, trying to protect them from destruction—for His mercy endures forever.

Jesus, the Source of Greatness

It humbles me to visualize the scene of brutal soldiers spitting on the Lord Jesus. I weep when I think of men hitting Jesus in the face and ripping out His beard. I am convicted when I hear Him say, "Father, forgive them; for they know not what they do" (Lk. 23:34). I ask myself, "What kind of love is this? What kind of man is this?" Jesus, the Son of the living God, showed us how to put down the sword.

When Jesus walked on the earth, He always walked in the protection of His Father because He was totally submitted in an attitude of humility and trust. It is only when we trust God in submission to Him that we receive His divine authority. If we want the power of God in our ministries, if we want to bear a costly anointing in our lives, then we must get under the authority of God's Word. His Word must become our final authority, our non-optional instruction, our only blueprint for living. It is our source of greatness.

Becoming Ministers of Mercy

After Tom and I got married and the honeymoon was over so to speak, there was a time when he stood up and basically told me that I was "out of line" in a certain area. I was offended by the manner he used to correct me. It wasn't what he said that bothered me, but how he had corrected me. I wanted to be instructed, not spanked! In fact, I hated it so much that I was asking myself, "Is this what love and marriage is all about? What's going on?" I got so ruffled that I started to become critical of him. I pointed my finger at him and said, "Why can't you be nicer in your discipline?"

Even though I may have been justified in my complaint against Tom's actions, I was so caught up in judgment toward him that I couldn't figure out why I didn't feel good about anything anymore. Circumstances seemed terrible and relationships began to crumble. Of course I was too smart to let the criticism come out of my mouth, but I was thinking it the whole time. I became critical of everybody and everything around me. Every time Tom shared something with me, it seemed to bother me. I continued to judge and point my finger until God said to me, "You are striving with your husband because you are afraid. You are lashing out in judgment because you are afraid, and I'm not going to protect you." Why did God say this to me? He would not protect me because I was walking in judgment and spiritual pride. God will never bless fear and pride. He won't bless your mess! He wants to clean us up. I had to learn that it is more important to be merciful than to be "right."

There are ways to overcome a judgmental and critical spirit that lingers in our lives. The Lord desires to cleanse His Church so we can truly be a chosen generation without spot or wrinkle.

Judge not, that ye be not judged. For with what judgment ye judge, ye shall be judged: and with what measure ye mete, it shall be measured to you again. And why beholdest thou the mote that is in thy brother's eye, but considerest not the beam that is in thine own eye? Or how wilt thou say to thy brother, Let me pull out the mote out of thine eye; and, behold, a beam is in thine own eye? Thou hypocrite, first cast out the beam out of thine own eye; and then shalt thou see clearly to cast out the mote out of thy brother's eye (Matthew 7:1-5).

Judgment is reserved for God. He says, "Vengeance is Mine; I will repay" (Rom. 12:19). When we use our tongues to cut others with judgmental words, that same "sword" will turn on us! We open the door for tormenting spirits to come into our lives, causing confusion and depression. Those under unjust attack are protected by God's mercy. Those leveling judgments at others will be exposed—that's right—exposed to the torments of evil spirits. **God lifts His protection unless we show mercy. If we sow judgment, we will reap judgment.**

If we want peace of mind, we must listen to God's Word: "The merciful man doeth good to his own soul" (Prov. 11:17a). If we want to be healed, happy, and carefree, we will show mercy to those who bruise us. If our hurt is so deep that we feel it every time someone touches us, then we must show mercy. (John Mason put it so well: "When you are kicked from behind, it must mean you are out in front.") Bask in God's love for you and let the healing begin.

When people point their fingers at us, and we reach out to them in love, our whole life turns around. Whenever anyone judges me, I say, "God, it may be my fault or it might not, but I sure

46

love him." Jesus said to pray for those who despitefully use you (see Mt. 5:44). Then rejoice that God sees you worthy of suffering because of the glory of God that rests upon you. It totally changes circumstances.

But why dost thou judge thy brother? or why dost thou set at nought thy brother? for we shall all stand before the judgment seat of Christ. For it is written, As I live, saith the Lord, every knee shall bow to Me, and every tongue shall confess to God. So then every one of us shall give account of himself to God. Let us not therefore judge one another any more: but judge this rather, that no man put a stumblingblock or an occasion to fall in his brother's way (Romans 14:10-13).

These are powerful, pointed words intended to get our thinking straight about judging other people. God basically tells us here "to mind our own business." We have enough to do just keeping ourselves submitted to God without having to help others do it too!

In Second Chronicles 35 we read about King Josiah, who felt it was his job to get involved with another king's war. Sometimes when we see others fighting or not doing things the way we think they should, we want to straighten them out and solve their problems. We use the sword of God's Word and play the part of the Holy Spirit to correct everyone's problems or issues. Don't meddle with God!

As we can see from this example, King Josiah found out that getting involved in someone else's affairs was the same as meddling with God's affairs.

After all this, when Josiah had prepared the temple, Necho king of Egypt came up to fight against Carchemish by Euphrates: and Josiah went out against him. But he sent ambassadors to him, saying, What have I to do with thee, thou king of Judah? I come not against thee this day, but against the house wherewith I have war: for God commanded me to make haste: forbear thee [refrain] *from meddling with God, who is with me, that He destroy thee not. Nevertheless Josiah would not turn his face from him, but disguised himself, that he might fight with him, and hearkened not unto the words of Necho from the mouth of God, and came to fight in the valley of Megiddo. And the archers shot at king Josiah; and the king said to his servants, Have me away; for I am sore wounded* (2 Chronicles 35:20-23).

Shortly after this Josiah died.

When we take the role of the Holy Spirit in people's lives, trying to bring conviction and direction, we have no real authority because it's not our place to do those things. Not only do we get in God's way of dealing with those people, but we also end up getting hurt ourselves. God alone delegates His authority to men and even then only as a representative of His Word. God's Word working through the Holy Spirit brings judgment. That is why intercession is the highest form of love you can offer others—because God alone can change the heart through the power of His Word.

Putting ourselves in a position of judging whether someone is right or wrong elevates us to the place of God's divine authority. The only way to get a place of judgment over a person's life is if we never break the law. We can compare actions or circumstances to the truth of God's Word, but the life of every person is in God's hands. Don't die like a stubborn, self-righteous king meddling in the affairs of others!

Speak not evil one of another, brethren. He that speaketh evil of his brother, and judgeth his brother, speaketh evil of the law, and judgeth the law: but if thou judge the law, thou art not a doer of the law, but a judge (James 4:11).

48

A number of passages from the Book of James have spoken louder to me than any I have ever read concerning this issue.

If you have been critical or judgmental toward others, now is the time to repent of your sin and receive God's mercy! Lay it before the altar in repentance and get rid of it because it may be stopping or blocking what God wants to do for you! "Grudge not one against another, brethren, lest ye be condemned: behold, the judge standeth before the door" (Jas. 5:9).

But the wisdom that is from above is first pure, then peaceable, gentle, and easy to be intreated, full of mercy and good fruits, without partiality, and without hypocrisy (James 3:17).

God's wisdom is easily entreated or persuaded. Do you have an open mind? Are you full of mercy and good fruits, without partiality or hypocrisy? The phrase *without partiality* means you don't set yourself apart or avoid someone because of some judgment or decree you've made about them.

God's wisdom allows us to associate with all people. It causes us to reach out our hand to all people and say, "I want to fellowship with you because we share a common Father and our spirits have been created by the Father God." God's wisdom (and mercy) is free of hypocrisy. We don't "put on" a false front, or show off; we mean what we say, and our actions line up with our words. Someone once said, "People who are always pointing fingers rarely hold out their hands" (to bless others).

The Abomination of Condemnation

The Body of Christ is infected with a self-destructive attitude that I call the "abomination of condemnation." We need to confront this demonic stronghold and, through the power and the grace of God, defeat it.

When I grew up, I never felt the pressure to perform a certain way to be accepted. I knew that I was loved just because I was Lori. If I made a mistake or sinned I was disciplined, but never rejected. After I began to fellowship in certain Christian circles, I experienced a level of legalism I had never known before. It was almost as if the people I met had higher standards for loving me than God did. What I discovered was that they were infected with this virus, "the abomination of condemnation."

This virus infects and affects many of the organs of the human body, but most importantly, the *heart*. Many of those infected also have problems with their *eyes*. When the eyes are infected, they begin to see everything that is wrong with people. When their eyes actually spot someone in a fault, their infected *mind* says, "We must keep sin *out* of our church, family, group, or organization!" The mind tells the infected person that it is their "end-time prophetic calling" in life to be the exposer of all that is not measuring up to the current move of God for today.

The *tongue* is extremely vulnerable to this virus. Because the tongue is so susceptible to infection, it is the easiest way to detect if a person has been infected. When the virus infects the tongue, it becomes quick to give reports about any alleged wrongdoing that it suspects about another. It is especially outspoken if the person is someone they are familiar with or is in a position of visibility, like a pastor or an evangelist. Familiarity seems to be a breeding ground for the abomination of condemnation virus.

I believe everyone in leadership needs to take a vow of confidentiality. It's sad to say, but the Church will never rise to victory if we do not learn the lesson of Mary the mother of Jesus. God revealed secret things to her *only* because she hid those precious words in her heart, pondering and meditating on them. We can do more damage to those who are closest to us by exposing failure even if we think it is for the right motivation. God says one of the things He hates most is the action of an individual who sows discord among the brethren (see Prov. 6:16-19). "He that covereth a transgression seeketh love; but he that repeateth a matter separateth *very* friends" (Prov. 17:9). "He that is of a faithful spirit concealeth the matter" (Prov. 11:13b).

The *feet* are also infected as they are told by the infected mind to go to as many people they can and warn them of the faults seen in others. Infected feet will go the extra mile to join the "crusade of correction" in order to remove any error or weakness out of their camp.

Of all the body parts that this virus infects, the one it damages most of all is the *heart*. When one is infected with the abomination of condemnation, it gives him or her a serious case of hardness of heart. An infected heart has little or no ability to help the hurting, heal the broken, and restore those who have been overtaken in a sin or a fault. Rather, the hardened heart believes that the wrongdoing it was able to discern so accurately is a reason for punishment or even abandonment of the individual. This of course is not a literal abandonment, but an emotional and spiritual abandonment.

The abomination of condemnation also affects our *attitudes*, not only about others, but also about ourselves. We become defensive and analytical, always blaming others for our own problems. This kind of infectious insecurity creates a judgmentalism of people, rather than a restoration of them. People with this virus "analyze" every problem on the basis of performance, without any thought of how the situation has influenced anyone other than themselves.

God has called all of us to be restorers of those who fall. The anointing God has given us is to restore those who are weak, not to crucify them. When we fail to use the anointing to restore, we end up rejecting people for the "right" reasons. The late Kathryn Kuhlman once said, "If you forgive, you are the biggest person on the face of this earth!" When you forgive, you step over into the offensive against the works of darkness in a person's life. God has chosen to deliver the human race through the power of forgiveness.

The Book of Job reveals what God will do in the end-time Church. Job was the first book of the Bible ever written; I believe God hides His endings in His beginnings. Job is a type of the end-time overcomer. Not only did he survive adversity, but he also learned how to minister restoration to others.

According to the Bible, Job was a perfect man (see Job 1:1). In the middle of his trials and troubles, Job's friends began to cry and weep with him. So far, so good. Right? Then a bad thing happened. Job began to open his heart up to them. He admitted that he had cursed the day he was born and had even said he didn't want to live anymore. The truth of Job's real feelings came out of his mouth. At that crucial point, Job's comforters were transformed into Job's accusers! First there was Eliphaz. His "goody two-shoes" philosophy questioned Job's righteousness and talked about all the things Job "should have done." He was trying to prove that since Job was suffering, he had sinned somehow.

Bildad was very narrow-minded. Job's second "friend," so to speak, saw all of life through methodical formulas and cause-and-effect patterns. In the situation that Job faced, these simplistic ideas of life just didn't work. People experiencing pain and distress need someone with a compassionate, restorative spirit to help them overcome those things.

Zophar was a professional fault-finder. He lectured poor Job. "If you just had enough faith, there would be no clouds." Job thought he could trust these men, so he revealed his inner secrets. In their eyes, here was their chance to pounce on a sinner and correct his ways! When people are hurting, their own suffering does not allow them to hear correction very much. They aren't able to hear "all the right answers." It's a matter of their heart, not their mind.

The Church of God is filled with fallible, flawed, fallen people who, like King David, are after God's own heart. They need to receive the "mercy of God" before they can receive the "laws of God."

Job was stripped of his status, his wealth, and even his family! When he desperately needed encouragement, he got criticism and correction. Still, God commanded Job to rise up. In the middle of his pain and the negative words of his "comforters," Job exploded with a burst of faith, declaring his heart:

Why do ye persecute me as God, and are not satisfied with my flesh? Oh that my words were now written! oh that they were printed in a book! That they were graven with an iron pen and lead in the rock for ever! For I know that my redeemer liveth, and that He shall stand at the latter day upon the earth (Job 19:22-25).

We've all heard it said, "If you can't say anything good about someone, don't say anything at all." God doesn't need any "Job's comforters" in the Church. Sin and pain are not automatically synonymous. We are instructed to minister to one another from the mercy seat in communion with God. God tells us in Exodus 25:22 that He will commune with us in one place and one place alone: the mercy seat! **When we don't live our lives in an attitude of mercy, we don't commune with God.** It's that simple.

It is uncomfortable to see people suffering and in pain. Sometimes it makes us feel like we need to have all the answers for them. The truth is, nobody has all the answers, only God does.

Job discovered the power in the sovereignty of God in Job 38:4. Whenever you are tempted to ask "Why, God? Why?" humble yourself. You should be grateful that you're not in charge of your life. When God asked Job some questions like, "Where were you when I laid the foundations of the earth?" or "Can you send lightnings that they may go and number the clouds in wisdom?" Job was dumbfounded. The secret things belong to God. You'd do better to not touch the secret things of God. You may enjoy picking people apart, but remember this: You only know a part of the story—if that! For all those who love to gossip—I say with no apology—get a life! Some folks are so insecure that they can't find anything better to do than rip people apart. God has little to do with those who are so proud and insecure that they feed on the human failures and deaths of others. Who wants to live the life of a Christian cannibal?

Instead, what we really need in our lives is the spirit of compassion and kindness that provides unconditional love. When we begin to pray for others, our own captivity will turn, just like Job's did.

If Jesus Himself learned obedience through the things that He suffered, why not us? God has not assigned us to remove the tares from His Church. So how do we deal with condemnation? As God told Job, "Gird up thy loins," rise up and declare, "If God be for us, who can be against us?" (Job 40:7; Rom. 8:31) The spirit of encouragement in you can put other people over the top to victory, and innoculate them against the virus of the abomination of condemnation! The power of God's positive Word over us as human beings is dynamic in its working.

The Body of Christ is designed to work together as a unified team. When one of the members of the Body suffers, we all suffer. When one of the members prospers, we are all blessed. If we don't have a restorative spirit in the Church, we literally condemn ourselves! We disqualify our own side from being able to win the war and complete the destiny God has on our lives. It's time to heed the words of Jesus when He says, "Put down the sword."

Chapter 5

The Ministry
of Encouragement

He climbs highest who helps another up. —Zig Ziglar

Great leaders, whether they are pastors, parents, coaches, or teachers, all have one thing in common. They are encouragers. Most people don't encourage themselves very much, so they have to depend on those around them for affirmation. The Body of Christ flourishes where the ministry of encouragement functions.

The Old Testament word for encouragement is *chazad*, which means "to build up, to strengthen, to fortify, or to restore." It speaks of an action done to something that already exists and needs repairing. It literally means "to restore something back to what it once had been." In the New Testament, encouragement implies building something that never even existed before. Under the Old Covenant, men had very little access to the presence of God, so they were constantly needing to be restored to fellowship with God through blood sacrifices. In the New Covenant, the single sacrifice of the Lamb of God sealed our relationship with the Father once and for all. Now He is constantly building, encouraging, and strengthening His people. He is actually building Himself a house to live in using His people.

The New Testament does not use the word *encouragement* in the same light as the Old Testament. In fact, the word *encouragement* is not used directly in the New Testament. Encouragement is defined by the words *edification*, *exhortation*, and *comfort*. The Bible says that prophecy is given to minister edification, exhortation, and comfort to the people of God. "But he that prophesieth speaketh unto men to edification, and exhortation, and comfort" (1 Cor. 14:3).

Words are powerful. Words can either build us up or tear us down. Words can make us feel very strong or they can leave us feeling so weak that we're left trembling, not knowing what to do or how to do it.

Encouragement Is Building God's House

God gave ministry gifts to the Body of Christ to speak words of encouragement and of life-giving instruction that will build us up. That is their primary function. Ephesians 4:12 (NKJ) describes these ministry gifts as "the equipping of the saints for the work of ministry, for the *edifying* of the body of Christ." The word *edification* in the New Testament means "to be a house-builder or constructor, as in a building." It refers to the work of building a dwelling place where workmen put all the parts together, laying the foundation and building up the walls. That's what God is doing in His Church when He edifies us; He's constructing and building us up! It's no coincidence that Jesus was a "carpenter's son."

The word *exhortation* means "to call near or compel by imparting a desire or motivation to someone." God is constantly calling

56

us near to Himself and near to one another so that together we will be the building He desires to live in. The Bible says that we are a "habitation of God through the Spirit" (Eph. 2:22). In order for the house to be complete, each part of the building is "fitly joined together and compacted by that which every joint supplieth" (Eph. 4:16). Each part of God's house is connected with a substance—a glue—that nothing can separate. That glue is the love of God!

Exhortation motivates people to work together, to be unified in heart and purpose. It creates a team mentality! That is how powerful the words we speak to someone can be. The very establishment of God's dwelling place in our midst is relative to the words we speak to one another. The Book of Proverbs says that "every wise woman buildeth her house" (Prov. 14:1a)! In God's house every part must be exhorted to join together on a consistent basis. In Hebrews 3:13 we are commanded to "exhort one another daily." That means to call them near to God by placing a desire in their heart for Him, rather than giving them a list of rules and laws to follow. It's easier to just yell at someone, telling him what to do, than to inspire that person to good works. **It takes the unconditional love of God to walk in the ministry of encouragement where others feel so strengthened that they are able to receive correction.** We must find ways to "stimulate" people to good works, not "scold" people to good works.

> ...*My son, despise not thou the chastening of the Lord, nor faint when thou art rebuked of Him: for whom the Lord loveth He chasteneth, and scourgeth every son whom He receiveth. If ye endure chastening, God dealeth with you as with sons; for what son is he who the father chasteneth not?* (Hebrews 12:5-7)

The word *chasten* means to correct in a disciplinary fashion. Chastening must occur for God to build His house correctly. But chastening usually occurs when folks can't hear a kind messenger. A part of exhortation may involve chastening. Exhortation means to compel others by imparting a motivation to them. For some the only motivation they heed is the threat of God's spanking.

Correction in a disciplinary fashion is necessary to build God's house, but it should never be delivered in anything but an encouraging spirit. Otherwise it brings forth death. When correction is administered with a spirit of anger or condemnation, it will cause discouragement to those who hear. "Fathers, provoke not your children to anger, lest they be discouraged" (Col. 3:21).

The word *comfort* means "to console by calling to one's side or giving comforting words of encouragement." When someone is down or has made a mistake, it may be hard for him or her to receive a word of correction. After comforting that person and operating in unconditional love, it is much easier for him or her to receive God's instruction. That's why God says we are to speak the truth "in love." Most anyone can point out where things are wrong or even what needs to be done. But to speak the truth in a spirit of love and meekness allows a measure of God's healing anointing to flow out of us. When that happens, there is no rejection in the rebuke. There is no disappointment in the discipline. People will more easily realize that they may have sinned, but won't feel condemned because of their sin. When they are really desirous of change and are drawn closer to God through the process, true edification, exhortation, and comfort have taken place.

...And the men of Israel put themselves in array to fight against them at Gibeah. And the children of Benjamin came forth out of Gibeah, and destroyed down to the ground of the Israelites that day twenty and two thousand men. And the people the men of Israel encouraged themselves... (Judges 20:20-22).

The men of Israel had made a decision to stand up for what was right, and it cost them dearly. They didn't understand why they had been defeated when God was on their side, but they refused to give up. They "encouraged themselves," built each other up, and were ready for battle again. Sometimes we get down in the dumps and feel too weary to go on. We simply need encouragement. Ultimately, on the third try, the men of Israel prevailed and removed sin from Israel. It wouldn't have happened if they had failed to encourage themselves.

The ministry of encouragement devastates the work of hell. It drives out darkness and eradicates the effects of evil. It acknowledges the finished work of Christ in our lives. We need to speak encouraging words over one another's lives so they will have strength and courage for the warfare. We are called to build up, strengthen, and encourage one another in the battle.

We are caught in a war, in a life-and-death struggle between the all-powerful forces of God and the dark forces of satan. Although we have no power in ourselves, we can rest in knowing that we serve Someone who is greater than the enemy we battle. The men of Israel encouraged themselves even after they suffered a setback. Things didn't look so great, and they had no guarantee that the next battle would go their way either, but they were filled with a righteous passion. They knew they were doing the right thing, and that God's purposes would ultimately triumph.

You and I need to have a holy fire and passion in our spirits! We need some holy anger about the devil's works! Let your righteous anger come out and use it to swing the sword of the Spirit against the enemy! I refuse to pamper the devil. He's killing people, taking our young, abusing our children, and stealing health and prosperity from the people of God. As you face your daily battles against darkness, you may feel down, depressed, and weary, but *one word of encouragement* can change your countenance and renew your strength! It will push back the dark forces of hell in your life.

We must have the ministry of encouragement to stay in the battle. If we don't, people will grow weak and weary, and fall away because they cannot fight it without encouragement. No one is an island unto himself. God really wants leaders to exercise and receive from the ministry of encouragement, so they, in turn, can speak it over their disciples.

Encouragement to Leaders

The members in the Body of Christ are responsible to bring the ministry of encouragement to their spiritual leaders. There are times when leaders get weak and need to hear words of encouragement to build them back up. Leaders need to have someone speak words of life to them or do a life-empowering deed that ministers healing and strength to their lives.

> *But charge Joshua, and encourage him, and strengthen him: for he shall go over before this people, and he shall cause them to inherit the land which thou shalt see* (Deuteronomy 3:28).

How can believers contribute to the word of God? How can every member of the Body become an extremely important part of God's building project? It is not only as you encourage one another, but even more powerfully as you minister to those in positions of headship: the leaders in the Body. They are the ones who are under the strongest attack. They are out in the forefront taking on the brunt of the warfare. They get pressure from all sides, hearing everyone's problems, being tempted by the devil and tested by God, undergoing trials from who knows where, plus feeling compassion for the lost and for others who are hurting.

Because these feelings can cause great weariness in our leaders, God says, "Encourage Joshua." Encourage your leaders. Let them know that they are doing a good job. Tell them how they have blessed you. Open yourself up once and a while and be vulnerable. Let leaders know that you're behind them (praying, not talking).

Build them up, strengthen them, and tell them something that will help. You may think that leaders don't need encouragement, but that's not true. You may think that leaders have it all together and don't need anyone. Wrong again. They need "the ministry of encouragement" *more* than anyone else. I know—I'm a leader. Leaders cannot do it by themselves. They'll grow weak and weary and will burn out before their time.

With the intense needs of leadership, each member of the Body needs to know what his or her role is. God says it is "to encourage, to build up, to strengthen, and to construct the house of God"! You may be a carpenter who goes throughout the place and hammers a nail here and throws up a piece of tile there. You may be vacuuming the carpet one day and cleaning the toilet the next. Whatever the role, we need to understand the importance of the ministry of helps and encouragement.

Encouragement in Operation

The apostle Paul gave us some beautiful examples of the ministry of encouragement in operation. He always encouraged the believers in his epistles before he asked them to change in any way. For example, he wrote:

> *Grace unto you, and peace, from God our Father and the Lord Jesus Christ. We are bound to thank God always for you, brethren, as it is meet, because that your faith groweth exceedingly, and the charity* [or the love] *of every one of you all toward each other aboundeth* (2 Thessalonians 1:2-3).

In the Book of Philemon, Paul wrote, "I thank my God, making mention of thee always in my prayers, hearing of thy love and faith, which thou hast toward the Lord Jesus, and toward all saints" (Philem. 4-5). Here are some positive words of encouragement from the apostle. He is saying, in effect, "Brothers and sisters, you bless me so much when I see how much you love each other and how much you trust in God. Keep up the great testimony of Christ's work in your lives and of being such a great example to the unbelievers." What an encouraging word to speak over someone. This is the ministry of encouragement in operation, of building up the Body of Christ. Without the ministry of encouragement, we wouldn't be able to regain our strength from day to day, or prepare for the next battle for lost souls.

Encouraging Yourself

David faced an impossible situation one day when literally everybody around him turned against him! A band of Amalekites captured the wives, family members, and property of David's entire army while they were away from home. When they found the smoking remains of their homes with no sign of their families, David and his men cried out so loudly and so long that they could cry no more!

And David was greatly distressed; for the people spake of stoning him, because the soul of all the people was grieved, every man for his sons and for his daughters: but David encouraged himself in the Lord his God (1 Samuel 30:6).

When no one gets in line to tell you what a great job you are doing, when no one seems to agree with your decision to obey God the best you can, what can you do? Do what David did: Encourage *yourself* in the Lord! When those you have loved and worked with just up and leave you, taking their support with them, what can you do? Encourage yourself in the Lord! When your family misunderstands you and your friends betray you, what do you do? Encourage yourself in the Lord! When those who have been your comrades in battle decide you are to blame for all their problems and pain, what do you do? Encourage yourself in the Lord! It's not an easy day when you have to face life's circumstances all alone in a whirlwind of rejection and accusation from those closest to you. To be great in God's Kingdom may require your going through some things alone—but with God's help.

Paul wrote to the Corinthians:

We are troubled on every side, yet not distressed; we are perplexed, but not in despair; persecuted, but not forsaken; cast down, but not destroyed; ... For we which live are alway delivered unto death for Jesus' sake, that the life also of Jesus might be made manifest in our mortal flesh (2 Corinthians 4:8-9,11).

Here is a man who throughout his writings is testifying to the fact that the encouragement of the saints got him through. In some situations, he had no one to encourage him but the Lord!

Here are some ways that might be helpful for you to encourage yourself in the Lord.

1. Review your victories. *Remember* some of the awards or trophies you have obtained. Look over them again. Get out the thank-you letters from those you have blessed over the years. *Read* over the testimonies of what God has done through your life and ministry. *Recall* the memories of God's working in your life to see how far you've come.

2. Remember your calling and mission from God. This will empower you with purpose and perseverance. Know that God has His hand on your life. Where God guides, He provides. Whom God appoints, He anoints. When we *review* the word of the Lord over our calling and ministry, it will build us up and strengthen us.

3. Rekindle your passion for intimacy with God. *Relationship* with Jesus and the Holy Spirit will bring a renewed sense of significance to your life. He loves you! He is for you, not against you. When He is for you, no one else can be against you. You are

God's very own possession, bought and paid for with the sacrifice of His Son. He will withhold no good thing from you. *Remember*, He is your first love!

4. Reward yourself by taking some time out for some enjoyment. *Relax* from the daily pressure of expectations facing you. *Rest* in the Lord's goodness and grace while you are regrouping.

5. Regroup in the areas that have been overlooked or that you are discouraged in. An evaluation of the neglected areas of our lives and callings should be done on an ongoing basis. *Reevaluate* the areas causing the discouragement to see what positive changes you could make.

6. Reaffirm the goals and vision God has given you to realize that the suffering is worth achieving the goal. You might find some goals that aren't so worthwhile that you can discard from your list. This will help you *recognize* just what you are supposed to be counting the cost for.

7. Remit the debts, offenses, and resentments you have accumulated in your life. Most of our discouragement comes from the injustices and disappointments we experience.

8. Renew your mind to what God says about your life and circumstances. Seeing things from God's viewpoint is always life-changing and empowering. Until we get God's perspective on our lives, we will always be overwhelmed with the impossibilities. Get *rejuvenated* with a fresh outlook from the throne of the Almighty!

May each of us be responsible to do our part to build up others. Let us strengthen our brothers and sisters in the faith and help them build the house of God. Don't let personal insecurity hinder the ministry of encouragement in your life. When you feel unworthy, when you are convinced that you have no grace or anointing to give to others, remember that God has need of each one of us!

I always minister best in those times when I am under the greatest attack. It is during those times that I know I have to trust in the Almighty God, because when I am weak, then He is strong. I realize that if anything is going to happen, it'll have to be God's doing! That may be your key to freedom and deliverance. If you feel weak, then know that God can then be strong for you and through you. The way to eradicate insecurity from your life is to live to give, not live to get.

Produce Fruit With Your Mouth

The ministry of encouragement to the Body of Christ helps those who are facing adversity or who are under the Lord's chastening to produce the "peaceable fruit of righteousness" in their lives (Heb. 12:11). If you are living a life of "performance" and measuring your "worth" by what you are doing, you will be in too much bondage to give your life to anybody. The Pharisees in Jesus' day had this same problem. They couldn't encourage anyone because they were so consumed with being "perfect" in the eyes of man.

God says to every believer, "I've given My life for you. I loved you that much, and I want to build you up every day. I want to encourage you to walk in the way." The life of God is in you. Now bring it forth by acknowledging every good thing that is in you in Christ Jesus (Philem. 6). Let them come out. As you begin to function in the good, you'll overcome the evil that's there. Trust is established as you encourage one another.

Let no corrupt communication [or speech] *proceed out of your mouth, but that which is good to the use of edifying* [or building up], *that it may minister grace unto the hearers* (Ephesians 4:29).

We must bridle our tongue and keep a watch over our mouth. The Book of Proverbs says, "In the multitude of words there wanteth not sin: but he that refraineth his lips is wise" (Prov. 10:19). The kind of ministry that God requires in this hour is very fine-tuned and Spirit-directed. He is fine-tuning us and teaching us that in the multitude of words, sin will abound.

A lot of people talk just because there is a lull in the conversation. The solution is simple: If you have nothing to say, don't talk. If you are trying to control the situation by your words, or make others feel comfortable by filling in the boring spots, cease from your own labors. God's Word says, "...In returning and rest shall ye be saved; in quietness and in confidence shall be your strength..." (Is. 30:15). We can rest quietly when we know there is a trust working among us. "He that refraineth his lips is wise" (Prov. 10:19b).

If you're not talking about something good, then simply be at peace. Let your life minister most powerfully by the character fruits of God's Spirit. Peace, love, and gentleness are better communicated by serving actions and personal presence than by spoken words. The Lord praises a woman who has a meek and quiet spirit in First Peter 3:4. He doesn't reward the loud, the "happy-go-lucky," or the so-called "carefree" woman who has the "gift of gab."

Sometimes the most effective encourager can be one who just stands quietly by and holds another's hand without saying a word. Let's learn when to speak and when to refrain from speaking. Let's become vessels that continually build up and strengthen the Body of Christ.

Part III

Humble Trust

Chapter 6

A Faceless Generation

Do you wish to be great? Then begin by being humble. Do you desire to construct a vast and lofty fabric? Think first about the foundation of humility. The higher your structure is to be, the deeper must be its foundation. —St. Augustine

The people of greatness that God is looking for today are called "a faceless generation." This faceless generation is so consumed in seeking the Lord's face that they no longer focus on His hand. Yes, His hand will always be there to guide, provide, and supply. But this generation has a goal to seek His face above all other things.

But we all, with open face beholding as in a glass the glory of the Lord, are changed into the same image from glory to glory, even as by the Spirit of the Lord (2 Corinthians 3:18).

The Psalmist wrote, "Seek the Lord, and His strength: seek His face evermore" (Ps. 105:4). When we stop trying to see so much of ourselves, we will see His face more clearly. If we are concerned about titles, positions, or promotions from men, we lose sight of the face of God and His approval.

In some cultures the expression "losing face" means an individual bears some sort of shame. Sometimes that could be the best thing that ever happened to us. When we can honestly say we are nothing apart from Him, then Christ becomes all in us. The Lord reveals the heart of this faceless generation in Matthew 6:1-6, when describing their life of hiddenness. When it comes to their spiritual activities, they don't do them to be seen or rewarded by men; they do them unto the Lord.

Take heed that ye do not your alms before men, to be seen of them: otherwise ye have no reward of your Father which is in heaven. Therefore when thou doest thine alms, do not sound a trumpet before thee, as the hypocrites do in the synagogues and in the streets, that they may have glory of men. Verily I say unto you, They have their reward. But when thou doest alms, let not thy left hand know what thy right hand doeth: that thine alms may be in secret: and thy Father which seeth in secret Himself shall reward thee openly. And when thou prayest, thou shalt not be as the hypocrites are: for they love to pray standing in the synagogues and in the corners of the streets, that they may be seen of men. Verily I say unto you, They have their reward. But thou, when thou prayest, enter into thy closet, and when thou hast shut thy door, pray to thy Father which is in secret; and thy Father which seeth in secret shall reward thee openly (Matthew 6:1-6).

On the other hand, Jesus also speaks of a people called a "generation of vipers." "But all their works they do for to be seen of men: they make broad their phylacteries, and enlarge the borders of their garments, and love the uppermost rooms at feasts, and the chief seats in the synagogues, and greetings in the markets, and to be called of men, Rabbi, Rabbi" (Mt. 23:5-7).

Jesus goes on to say to these vipers:

But be not ye called Rabbi: for one is your Master, even Christ; and all ye are brethren. And call no man your father upon the earth: for one is your Father, which is in heaven. Neither be ye called masters: for one is your Master, even Christ. But he that is greatest among you shall be your servant. And whosoever shall exalt himself shall be abased; and he that shall humble himself shall be exalted. ... Ye serpents, ye generation of vipers, how can ye escape the damnation of hell? Wherefore, behold, I send unto you prophets, and wise men, and scribes: and some of them ye shall kill and crucify; and some of them shall ye scourge in your synagogues, and persecute them from city to city (Matthew 23:8-12,33-34).

Just as these religious leaders were ambitious and hungry for positions of power in Jesus' day, so this same attitude can seduce many in the Church today. God forbid that we seek titles and positions for the praises of men rather than to serve for the glory of God. The opinions of men can take the attention away from the purpose of God. Knowing the right ministers and marketing the right ministries can become a goal in and of itself. Even the pursuit of purpose can be prostituted for advancing one's own lifestyle of greed and glory. A mixture of servanthood and selfishness does not go over big with the King of this faceless generation.

The people of this faceless generation are first and foremost worshipers and then warriors. That means we start out seeking the face of God giving Him our thanks, appreciation, and admiration. Second, we destroy the works of the enemy by proclaiming our faith in God's Word and our commitment to an unselfish lifestyle of faithful service.

A confident assurance lives deep within the hearts of this faceless generation. They know their God and are strong in the power of His might. They rest not on their own ability to get things accomplished, but on God's ability to do His work through their yielded life. They know that God will use the gifts He has given them when and how it pleases Him. A divine rest and peace consumes these faceless partners of God's Kingdom. They do not rejoice when others see *their* face, but when others see the face of God smiling through human flesh.

One day a despairing monk cried out to God, requesting to be set free from his performance-based religion. He loved God, but felt incapable of pleasing Him. God gave Martin Luther a revelation of Romans 3:28, which says, "Therefore we conclude that a man is justified by faith without the deeds of the law." It was then that the Great Reformation started in the Church. The revelation that changed the world forever was simple—God grants us grace and faith to overcome. It put mankind back on track with God's plan to be a faceless generation.

Like Martin Luther, I have spent many sleepless nights wondering if I had done enough to accomplish my God-given goals. When I realized that all my striving for greatness got me nowhere with God, I looked into the face of Jesus and found true peace. "Therefore being justified by faith, we have peace with God through our Lord Jesus Christ" (Rom. 5:1).

Take a look at Peter, the mighty apostle who changed the complexion of the world he lived in. At one point his ambitions got him so worked up that he cut a man's ear off. This shows how zeal without knowledge, or ambition without humility, can be a very deadly thing: "If someone gets in our way we'll just cut 'em up, bless God!" Thank God Peter found grace after looking into the forgiving eyes of Jesus. When the cock crowed and Peter had denied Jesus for the third time because of the opinions of men, Jesus looked straight into Peter's heart and changed him forever.

The faceless generation will be consumed with this one desire, that all should see the character and the face of Jesus. For others to see Him in us, we must be hidden in Him. Sometimes we want to hide Him in our heart as if He's our little secret. You know what I mean: "Me and Jesus got this little thing going, but I'm not about to tell anyone about it!" However, Jesus doesn't want to be *hidden* in us; He wants to be *seen* in us. When Jesus' character is worked in us we have a desire not to be seen of men, but to spotlight the magnificent love of God.

A faceless generation will not seek the attention of others through insecurity or pride. They are secure in God's love and humbly trust Him for their affirmation and reward. Safety or security can never fully be found in any person, place, or thing. My mother-in-law once said, "If it takes anything but Jesus to make you happy, then you've got a god on your hands and it must come down." God commands us to burn our idols and put Him first above everything else. It's only in the "secret place" that real security is found. That is where the face of Jesus is engraved on our life. When we dwell in the secret place with Jesus, there is tremendous encouragement and peace. The faceless generation represents true humility born of the Spirit.

True Humility

Someone once said, that it was pride that changed angels into devils, but it is humility that makes men like angels. Jonah found humility in the belly of a fish. Jacob discovered it during a wrestling match. Joseph learned it in a desert pit. Moses learned it in the wilderness. Samson found it in a harlot's lap. David rediscovered it through his sin. Solomon had to repeat the lesson even with all his wisdom. Heathen kings learned it at the hands of Israelite prophets like Isaiah and Daniel. The apostle Paul learned it through a blinding light. Jesus epitomized it from His birth to His sacrificial death on the tree. If we want to be wise, we will learn humility from God's Word rather than from the hard and painful path of experience!

Life is too short to have to learn everything by our own mistakes. The highest way to God's revelation knowledge is for us to humble ourselves. God honors humility and rejects pride. By walking humbly before Him, we receive His wisdom and direction for our lives. If we continue to walk in this manner, such wisdom will be poured out into our lives that others around us will want to follow and receive God's blessings. A life that learns to please God through true humility will be a life that God's greatness is seen in. It is a life that can discern and responds to the needs of others. The humble before God may not be all that able. But because of their availability, God empowers them with ability.

The Hebrew word *anavah* is translated as "humility, gentleness, or meekness." This word appears in Proverbs 15:33: "The fear of the Lord is the instruction of wisdom; and before honour is humility." The writer also describes humility from another perspective: "Before destruction the heart of man is haughty, and before honour is humility" (Prov. 18:12). Before God honors you, He teaches you what humility is. If you don't learn God's lesson, ultimate destruction is sure to follow. The rewards for mastering these lessons are unfathomable! The Bible tells us, "By humility and the fear of the Lord are riches, and honour, and life" (Prov. 22:4).

Riches, honor, and life are what most people think life is all about! Wouldn't you like to have these blessings abounding in your life? In the United States, people believe that the pursuit of these things is a basic human right. Most people, however, don't have the first clue as to how to obtain such godly blessings in their lives. That's because they are not obtained through the obvious means of man's natural, earthly ability. This is the pursuit of something most people don't think is important or even desirable for their life. The very idea of going down in order to be on top is ludicrous. The concept of doing little things to be big and small things to be great is repulsive to the natural mind. Why bother serving those who can do nothing for you? However, it is the only way God's Kingdom works, whether we agree with it or not.

In the New Testament, the Greek word for "humility" is *tapeinophrosune*. That is a mouthful, but it means lowliness or humbleness of mind. Many people think they are humble if they put themselves down with their words or actions or think poorly of themselves. **The truth is that we are automatically humbled and walk in humility when we see ourselves in the light of His character and greatness.** Some of the difficulties in walking out humility take place because we don't realize that all of us deserve nothing but hell! It seems as if that is where the rubber meets the road, so to speak.

In the Book of Acts, the apostle Paul testified, "...I have been with you at all seasons, serving the Lord with all *humility of mind*, and with many tears, and temptations, which befell me..." (Acts 20:18-19). Paul was describing how he served the Lord with humility of mind right in the middle of opposition, betrayal, and rejection by others. Humility is related to overcoming temptation, adversity, and injustice.

If you walk in humility, there is no way the plan of God for your life can be defeated. God has openly declared, "Before honor comes humility." Paul was pressed and stressed many times in his life and ministry. The cares of the Church weighed heavily on his shoulders night and day. Many people misunderstood him—even abandoned him and rejected him. He didn't have the comforts of a spouse to support and help him. He was a man alone. He was a man who was consumed with a purpose and a mission. As long as the anointing and grace of God were with him, he knew he could make it.

Paul began as a highly educated, respected Pharisee who was probably groomed for a high position of leadership over Israel by the most respected and wealthy men in his nation. His religious zeal was legendary around the Jewish world. He left it all behind him after Jesus confronted him on the road to Damascus. Something miraculous happened in his life that day that continued in the years he spent alone with God in the desert. God knocked Paul off his high horse! As he was on a mission to persecute the Christians, Jesus literally knocked Paul off a horse and His presence was revealed to him in a blinding light. God's presence created a humility in Paul that brought him to the point where he could say, "But by the grace of God I am what I am..." (1 Cor. 15:10).

Meekness is defined as power under control. Jesus Christ was meek, but there has never been a more powerful man on this earth! He was God incarnate, the living Son of God, Lord of lords, and King of kings. All power was given to Him, yet He was so meek that He willingly submitted to crucifixion on a tree. "...He was led as a sheep to the slaughter; and like a lamb dumb before his shearer, so opened He not His mouth" (Acts 8:32).

In discussing meekness, I am reminded of the spirited stallion in the feature motion picture, *Black Stallion*, who was so powerful that he was virtually unbeatable. He also defied the best efforts of men on two continents to tame him—until he submitted to the love of a small boy. This is a perfect picture of what the New Testament Greek words, *prautes* and *praotes*, mean. Both forms of the term are translated as "meekness."

This stallion was neither weak nor mild; he was untamed and incredibly powerful. He had all the instincts of a wild stallion, including the drive to resist to the death every effort to tame him. The key point is that the Black Stallion willingly submitted every wild instinct and fear to the hand of the boy. He chose to be meek for the sake of love.

Humility Is a Spiritual Attitude

Humility is not simply lowly compliance. **Humility is an attitude of submission to the Spirit.** God has invested immeasurable power and potential in each of us, along with the gifts, abilities, and skills we need to help us fulfill that potential. We will never fulfill our destinies by merely relying on these things, however. When we willingly lay down our strengths and admit our weaknesses, yielding the reigns of our lives to the hand of God, we can *then* tap our potential in Christ. When we are meek we will inherit the earth (see Mt. 5:5).

> *Then Paul answered, What mean ye to weep and to break mine heart? for I am ready not to be bound only, but also to die at Jerusalem for the name of the Lord Jesus* (Acts 21:13).

Paul's friends and brethren begged him to avoid the enemies and probable death that awaited him in Jerusalem. With a simple choice to avoid one city, this man could have avoided an early death and lived a long life of relative peace. He was intelligent, well-trained, respected, and established in the growing Church. He had already willingly given up his old security in the Jewish world for the sake of Christ. Now he was willingly giving up his security in the Christian world for the sake of love. He was purposely placing his neck in the noose of those who were wrongly accusing him—all for the opportunity to somehow reach some of his countrymen. He chose to follow in the footsteps of his Savior, even if it meant certain death. **This is an example of true biblical meekness—having controlled strength and submitted obedience—in the face of danger, misunderstanding, and perhaps even death.** Meekness has nothing to do with weakness!

The first test of a truly great man is his humility. I do not mean by humility, doubt of his own power. But really great men have a curious feeling that the greatness is not in them, but through them. And they see something divine in every other man and are endlessly, foolishly, incredibly merciful. —John Ruskin

Unlike the authority structures and political systems of the world, the Body of Christ is fueled by love and "oiled" by the supernatural virtue of submissive meekness. The Church is neither a democracy nor a dictatorship run by men. It is a theocracy ruled by God Himself, with a divine delegation of undershepherds who function as servant-leaders in God's grace. Nothing ordained by God will be done with "the arm of flesh." Meekness is vital in the work and functioning of the Church.

Jesus' Example of Meekness

Once again, there is no greater example of meekness in human relationships and ministry than in the life of Jesus Christ. From the beginning, the Son of God was clothed in meekness.

For what the law could not do, in that it was weak through the flesh, God sending His own Son in the likeness of sinful flesh, and for sin, condemned sin in the flesh (Romans 8:3).

This same God/man, who was clothed in the "likeness of sinful flesh," never sinned. He was sure of His destiny on the far side of the cross, and sure of His identity with His Father. This meek Man was the same Man who whipped the moneychangers and sellers of doves and bodily threw them out of the temple! (See Matthew 21:12.)

This is the same man who challenged and defeated the finest and most powerful minds of Israel's elite Sanhedrin in every confrontation. This is the man who refused to answer the Roman authority who thought he had the power of life and death over Jesus (even though His silence ensured Him a place on Calvary's tree).

This isn't a picture of weakness—it is a portrait of the world's most powerful man wrapped in the attitude of true spiritual *meekness*!

Jesus also demonstrated true meekness by the way He dealt with other people. When the Pharisees and doctors of the law tried to entrap Jesus in a surefire scheme involving the Law of Moses and an absolutely guilty victim, Jesus used *meekness* to overcome and accomplish His purpose.

And the scribes and Pharisees brought unto Him a woman taken in adultery; and when they had set her in the midst, they say unto Him, Master, this woman was taken in adultery, in the very act. Now Moses in the law commanded us, that such should be stoned: but what sayest Thou? This they said, tempting Him, that they might have to accuse Him. But Jesus stooped down, and with His finger wrote on the ground, as though He heard them not. So when they continued asking Him, He lifted up Himself, and said unto them, He that is without sin among you, let him first cast a stone at her. And again He stooped down, and wrote on the ground. And they which heard it, being convicted by their own conscience, went out one by one, beginning at the eldest, even unto the last: and Jesus was left alone, and the woman standing in the midst. When Jesus had lifted up Himself, and saw none but the woman, He said unto her, Woman, where are those thine accusers? hath no man condemned thee? She said, No man, Lord. And Jesus said unto her, Neither do I condemn thee: go, and sin no more (John 8:3-11).

Jesus stooped down to the ground right in front of His enemies. He stripped Himself of dignity and put Himself even lower than they were. Then He silently wrote in dirt something that convicted them of their own hypocritical lives. This turned the tables on them in a way none of them ever dreamed! **Meekness has a way of**

convicting hypocrites, silencing critics, and bringing to light the true ways of God.

Rejoice greatly, O daughter of Zion; shout, O daughter of Jerusalem: behold, thy King cometh unto thee: He is just, and having salvation; lowly, and riding upon an ass, and upon a colt the foal of an ass (Zechariah 9:9).

The Lord quietly fulfilled all the ancient prophecies concerning the Messiah—including the passages that the learned religious leaders had carefully avoided because they didn't fit into their preconceived theologies and agendas. Most of the leaders in Jesus' day just couldn't see the Messiah, the One they hoped would deliver them from the harsh rule of the Roman Empire. They couldn't fathom the Messiah arriving on a jackass without an army or a sword. But, the Messiah had come, and He came armed with *meekness.*

Some Christians today are not comfortable thinking of Jesus as living a life of suffering on this earth and enduring the shame of a criminal's death. Even more uncomfortable to them seems to be this command that He gave "to leave all and follow" in His footsteps. Follow His example and embrace the suffering and persecution that goes along with being one of His followers. They have enough problems; they don't need this besides!

Rather, it is much easier to adopt the "King's Kid" mentality that says, "I am a joint heir with Jesus; therefore, everything just belongs to me." Everyone else, well, they can just claim their own inheritance, I guess. But Jesus has called His followers to a much higher level of Christian lifestyle than to be just grabbing for whatever they need, as if God is some infidel who is not able to provide for His own. Yes, we are the heirs of His Kingdom. But that inheritance is to be given away so others might know the goodness and blessings of God's Kingdom. His Kingdom purpose is to be sought first—provisions follow. Jesus said, "Heal the sick, cleanse the lepers, raise the dead, cast out devils: freely ye have received, freely give" (Mt. 10:8).

I can of Mine own self do nothing: as I hear, I judge: and My judgment is just; because I seek not Mine own will, but the will of the Father which hath sent Me. If I bear witness of Myself, My witness is not true (John 5:30-31).

A beautiful example of humility is in Jesus' attitude of complete representation toward His Father. He never did anything He didn't see His Father do, or say anything He didn't hear His Father say. This is an essential lesson for any student who is trying to be like his or her teacher. We can never be leaders until we have learned to be followers. Many of us have learned to be "independent thinkers," so when we carry out instructions, we do it our own way. Leaders who think this way lead by control, not by godly example. Substituting our own ideas or will in the place of what God has told us to do, stems from pride and independence. The "sin of iniquity" puts the "I will" on the throne of our lives rather than "His will."

This is what I call "Burger King Christianity," a Christianity where you want to "have it your way." We want to live in the Kingdom, but we don't want the Kingdom to live in us. We want to go to Heaven, but we don't want to die to get there. We seek all the blessings and advantages of the Kingdom, but we look for the "blue light special" or a "kingdom clearance." We like the microwave ministry where we can receive instant freedom from the consequences of our sin with a "special miracle" or a gift of healing. We reason, "God is a God of love and grace," forgetting that God doesn't exempt Himself from His own laws of sowing and reaping. God can supersede the laws of sowing and reaping with a miracle of mercy, but God's highest way of working in this earth is through seedtime and harvest. Notice that between "seed" and "harvest" there is *time*. Time for what? Time for humble faithfulness.

Substitution seems like the normal attitude for many prideful twentieth-century Christians. We've been told "you can have it your way" for so long, we think our churches should do it our way too! In fact, if our church doesn't do things the way we think...well, there's always another drive-thru ministry around the corner where I can just order the Sunday message, give an offering, and be on my way...hold the conviction please! We have been programmed to buy what will satisfy momentarily rather than for eternity. What happened to commitment, covenant, and faithfulness? Are these too old-fashioned?

The majority of life revolves around the laws of sowing and reaping. The situations you live in today are a result of your own doing—your own choices. God is never to blame for evil. Meekness takes responsibility by accepting the consequences of wrong choices. Meekness also trusts that God, who is gracious, can bring redemption through His Word, turning even that which was meant for our evil around for our good.

True humility is submitted strength that represents the Father's plan. Jesus possessed power, wisdom, and might in His own right, yet He willingly laid it all aside to serve His Father. He only spoke the words His Father gave Him to speak. He submitted to the will of the Father over and above the will of His own flesh. Though His body didn't want to die, He yielded to His Father's will and accepted the bitter cup of death to save the guilty sons and daughters of Adam.

Jesus constantly prayed and communed with His Father. Although He was fully God, He was also fully man. He was subject to human weaknesses like fatigue and hunger. That is why the angels were sent to minister to Him after His 40-day ordeal and His confrontation with satan in the wilderness (see Mt. 4:11). Humility has two sides to it. Humility includes the attitude that says, "I recognize my inability and the fact that I cannot do anything without God." Yet it also submits and believes that "With God I can do all things."

Meekness has its confidence in God. The meek man and woman have a hiding place of unshakable security with God. God loves to honor the meek. Jesus literally promised, "Blessed are the meek: for they shall inherit the earth" (Mt. 5:5). A genuinely meek person never compares him or herself with others. Jesus constantly instructed His disciples to measure themselves against God's standard of meekness, not each other.

Meekness Marks Great Leaders

Elisha was the prophet we remember as "the man who received a double portion." The strange thing about Elisha is that the Bible remembers him for another reason. When a powerful king was searching for a prophet to hear from God, Elisha was described in a totally different way. Nothing was said of the double portion, or of water parting in a miracle. Elisha was marked by a sign of *meekness*:

> *But Jehoshaphat said, Is there not here a prophet of the Lord, that we may enquire of the Lord by him? And one of the king of Israel's servants answered and said, Here is Elisha the son of Shaphat, **which poured water on the hands of Elijah**. And Jehoshaphat said, The word of the Lord is with him. So the king of Israel and Jehoshaphat and the king of Edom went down to him* (2 Kings 3:11-12).

How would you feel if you were known as "the one who poured water on the hands of Billy Graham"? Perhaps you would prefer a recommendation like this: "Oh, that's the one who preached in Africa and saw 10,000 souls saved in one afternoon!" The fact is that Elisha was recognized more for his meekness and faithfulness than for his miraculous ministry (and he did have a miraculous ministry!).

*And Jehu the son of Nimshi shalt thou anoint to be king over Israel: and **Elisha the son of Shaphat of Abelmeholah shalt thou anoint to be prophet in thy room**. And it shall come to pass, that him that escapeth the sword of Hazael shall Jehu slay: and **him that escapeth from the sword of Jehu shall Elisha slay**. Yet I have left me seven thousand in Israel, all the knees which have not bowed unto Baal, and every mouth which hath not kissed him. So he departed thence, and found Elisha the son of Shaphat, who was plowing with twelve yoke of oxen before him, and he with the twelfth: and Elijah passed by him, and cast his mantle upon him* (1 Kings 19:16-19).

God will only entrust the powerful discernment of a prophet with men and women who are meek! God deeply values meekness in His servants. It is one of the most important requirements for greatness in His Kingdom. Meekness shows up in the character of every great person in the Bible. In nearly every case, meekness was developed in their lives through adversity rather than being resident through birth. Many times, meekness is confused with weakness by collaborators and associates. Moses ran into this problem with his own family members.

And they said, Hath the Lord indeed spoken only by Moses? hath He not spoken also by us? And the Lord heard it. (Now the man Moses was very meek, above all the men which were upon the face of the earth.) And the Lord spake suddenly unto Moses, and unto Aaron, and unto Miriam, Come out ye three unto the tabernacle of the congregation. And they three came out (Numbers 12:2-4).

Miriam and Aaron made the big mistake of comparing themselves with Moses. They didn't realize that God's calling and anointing have almost nothing to do with personal ability or qualifications. He loves to transform plain, ordinary men and women

84

into extraordinary miracle-workers and leaders. When these ministers are meek, then He receives all the glory. When they are proud, they set themselves up for a fall. Aaron was the brother of Moses, and Miriam was his sister. They forgot the supernatural side of leadership and began to be offended by the honor Moses was receiving from God. One of the things God respects most is folks who can honor the anointing on leaders' lives without falling into the sin of familiarity. Miriam and Aaron, though, began to murmur to themselves, forgetting that God "hears" every word spoken in the open or in secret.

And He said, Hear now My words: If there be a prophet among you, I the Lord will make Myself known unto him in a vision, and will speak unto him in a dream. My servant Moses is not so, who is faithful in all Mine house. With him will I speak mouth to mouth, even apparently, and not in dark speeches; and the similitude of the Lord shall he behold: wherefore then were ye not afraid to speak against My servant Moses? And the anger of the Lord was kindled against them; and He departed (Numbers 12:6-9).

The goal of the humble is to own a servant's towel, not a king's scepter. The humble ask, "What can I do to make someone else succeed and be great?" The apostle Paul gave this warning to the Galatians:

For, brethren, ye have been called unto liberty; only use not liberty for an occasion to the flesh, but by love serve one another. For all the law is fulfilled in one word, even in this; Thou shalt love thy neighbour as thyself. But if ye bite and devour one another, take heed that ye be not consumed one of another (Galatians 5:13-15).

The Holy Spirit does not manifest Himself through vessels that are partial to favorites, condescending, or filled with independence. He seeks meek vessels who have submitted all their strengths, dreams, and abilities to the hand of Almighty God. Then it is His delight to honor and exalt the meek to a place of power and authority in the earth.

With our divine destiny of greatness may come roads that don't always look like they're going in the right direction. When thoughts of greatness first enter our mind they seem to tempt us with feelings of comfort, security, or popularity. But, as we have seen, greatness in the Kingdom of God is not that way. That is why an attitude of "humble trust" in God's divine purpose for our lives is essential.

Disciplines and Fruits of Humility

Likewise, ye younger, submit yourselves unto the elder. Yea, all of you be subject one to another, and be clothed with humility: for God resisteth the proud, and giveth grace to the humble. Humble yourselves therefore under the mighty hand of God, that He may exalt you in due time: casting all your care upon Him; for He careth for you (1 Peter 5:5-7).

It is extremely important that we recognize both the "disciplines and fruits" of humility. Peter begins by telling the young to submit to their elders, but then he applies his anointed exhortation to *every believer*! All of us—baby believers, seasoned believers, laymen, preachers, men, women, black, white, grandparents, and teens—we are all to be subject one to another! In fact, he commands us to "be clothed with humility." If that sounds drastic, understand that it *is drastic* because of the *drastic consequences* if we fail to do what he says!

Our survival as an effective Church in the earth depends on our becoming that faceless generation walking in unity as one Body. Jesus said, "By this shall all men know that ye are My disciples, if ye have love one to another" (Jn. 13:35). This next statement is of supreme importance. The reason we must clothe ourselves with humility is so we may be united as one body. Humility enables us to hear another person. If we spend so much time preserving our own ideas and opinions we will never be open to *hearing* from another person. Unless we hear one another, we can never receive the revelation of *Christ*, which is the only thing that can unite us.

Where does God command the blessing? Where will God command the blessing in the years to come? The blessing is commanded by God where brothers live together in unity! Psalm 133 says, "Behold, how good and how pleasant it is for brethren to dwell together in unity! ...for there the Lord commanded the blessing, even life for evermore" (Ps. 133:1,3).

As we walk humbly before God and toward people, there comes an ability to peacefully work through the conflicts, challenges, differences, and disagreements that would normally tear us apart. By considering others as better or more important than ourselves, we can face situations with tremendous benefit and growth. God considers humility in relationships to be so essential that without it, He will not give His blessing.

Those who humble themselves are destined for greatness and promotion in God's Kingdom.

...for God resisteth the proud, and giveth grace to the humble. Humble yourselves therefore under the mighty hand of God, that He may exalt you in due time (1 Peter 5:5-6).

Humility recognizes our dependency not only on God, but also on one another. It knows that God has placed different gifts, abilities, and talents in each individual and that we all have need of one another. It understands that each person has some strengths and some weaknesses and that where one is weak, the other is strong. The Lord's design of the Church is such that we all must depend on one another in some area or another. This loving submission is the result of a humble attitude acknowledging God's callings and choices over people's lives. The humble person is quick to receive from others' giftings and to encourage them to step out in faithful service.

Some people claim that Christianity is for weak people who need a crutch. I say, "Give me two crutches! In fact, I'll just let God carry me where He wants me, even to places I don't want to go!" **One of the most important disciplines and fruits of humility is a total dependency on God.** Independent people usually have handicapped faith. Their determination to lean on their own weak flesh, limited intellect, and even past victories, is a guaranteed prescription for burnout and bitterness! True joy and fulfillment come when humility and patience have their perfect work, making you totally dependent upon God and trusting in the finished work of Christ. Remember, you can even do a good thing for too long. When God requires change, good things may not be God's things! It takes humility to hear God.

Independent people are usually proud people. They take pride in their ability to "do it on their own." God's best is for us to be dependent on Him and interdependent on people. Each member of the Body of Christ needs the other members, but each of us is fully equipped to fellowship directly with God without any human intermediary or priest to "speak and hear for us." That is the irony and glory of our salvation in Christ.

It is extremely important to teach our children to be dependent on God, while learning to be independent of worldly counsel and ungodly criticism. It is important for them to discover that Mommy and Daddy have some answers to their questions. An emphasis on humility teaches them to depend on God's wisdom in His Word, even throughout their adulthood. It also keeps them from being conceited.

One of the greatest disciplines to help us conquer pride is to purposely take the lowest place in public situations! When we "take the lowest seat" in any given situation, or when we give to those who can give nothing back, we discipline ourselves to walk in humility.

Jesus said:

When thou art bidden of any man to a wedding, sit not down in the highest room; lest a more honourable man than thou be bidden of him; and he that bade thee and him come and say to thee, Give this man place; and thou begin with shame to take the lowest room. But when thou art bidden, go and sit down in the lowest room; that when he that bade thee cometh, he may say unto thee, Friend, go up higher: then shalt thou have worship in the presence of them that sit at meat with thee. For whosoever exalteth himself shall be abased; and he that humbleth himself shall be exalted (Luke 14:8-11).

If we are struggling with pride in any area, let's remember the counsel of Jesus and "take the lowest room [or seat]." Pride will quickly "lose its place" in our lives! When you are on the job, prefer somebody else in love. When you are dealing with your spouse, shock him or her and "take the lower seat" by preferring your mate's happiness or choice over your own.

If we are wise enough to humble *ourselves* before the mighty hand of God, then God will exalt us rather than humble us through correction. "Putting ourselves down" for the ulterior motive of getting something from God is not humility; that's false humility and manipulation. Allow the will of God to rule your life for no other reason than the fact that it is the will of God. Humility seeks no other reward than to be like Jesus. If you are humble (and secure in your relationship with God), you will be able to learn something from everyone you meet in life—even your "worst enemy."

Humility Before Others

The fruit or discipline of humility also affects our relationship with other believers. People who have never submitted to the discipline of humility are often strong-willed or dogmatic. Humility is a virtue that continually develops in us through the tempering of God, the dealings of the Holy Spirit, and those life experiences that teach us the principle that we do not live for ourselves, but for the benefit of others.

Did you know that without humility, we can't even receive God's Word? Consider this Scripture: "...receive with meekness the engrafted word, which is able to save your souls" (Jas. 1:21). My mother-in-law is a lovely, wise old saint of God. I deeply respect her insights because I know she honors God's Word above her own opinions. She literally prayed every one of her family members, including her husband, into the Kingdom of God. She once said something so powerful that I have never forgotten it. She said her hunger for God led her to humble herself and pray, "Now God, I know there's more to being a Christian than I'm experiencing, but I don't know what it is. I ask that You take away all my preconceived ideas about You. Allow me to have what You call *humility*." She got what she prayed for. Her life was never the same.

Humility is the fruit of a spirit that says, "Lord, I'm a natural nothing, but with You and Your Word, I can be a supernatural something. You can take my weakness and change it into strength. You can take my worthlessness and produce something of value. You can take my insignificance and turn it into greatness."

Dogmatic, opinionated, and legalistic ideas are a form of pride that masquerades as religious devotion. Once a doctrine or opinion becomes so important to you that you cannot respect any person who challenges it or shares another idea with you, it has become a deterrent to the plan of God! In other words, when you value your ideas more than the personhood of another human being, then pride has overtaken you.

"But I have to defend the truth of God!" some say. You mean defend the reputation of an all-powerful God? There is a place to defend our faith and give account for our beliefs, but we should never downgrade or condemn another person over these things. God's truth cannot be changed by another person's words, but the person will almost certainly be changed by your steadfast love and confident humility in the face of his or her anger or erroneous statements. The apostle Paul faced constant opposition, but he stayed in the Spirit and patiently presented the truth from week to week wherever he was. Jesus did attack the Pharisees, for they were religious hypocrites who should have known better than to condemn God's people with their own traditions.

Once you have humbled yourself before God, your ideas and opinions will come across much softer. Instead of declaring, "Well, the only way you can do that is...," you will say without pride or boastfulness, "In my experience with God, I've seen God do this...." You will no longer feel you need to "prove your point" to everybody. In all cases, it is far better and more important to be kind than to prove yourself right.

We need to learn as a corporate body how to humble ourselves before the Lord in prayer and say, "Lord, what do You want from us? Our lives are Yours to command." That is the discipline of humility. "I'll be patient. I'm not going to get out ahead of You, Lord; I am going to wait on You until Your grace guides me into Your will." **The humble believer gets on his or her face before God and continually seeks God's wisdom and guidance in order to do His will.** Those believers always remember that it's better to be a little behind God than out ahead! If you're behind Him, He'll cover you. If you are out ahead of Him, you'll face the blows alone.

Humility is essential to your spiritual growth, as well as to unity in the Church universal. The Gospel of John records the final prayer of our Savior as He prepared to die. It has been said that a dying man's prayer is the most important thing on his heart. Jesus cried out for love and unity in His Church. He prayed, "That they all may be one; as Thou, Father, art in Me, and I in Thee, that they also may be one in Us: that the world may believe that Thou hast sent Me" (Jn. 17:21).

This bears repeating. **We can only be one to the degree that we walk in humility toward one another and toward God.** Humility allows us to really hear one another, causing us to work together. God asks us to value one another as people, more than we value our petty desires, inflated egos, or "personal rights." The Church has been terribly marred and crippled by our inability to work together because of divisions over petty issues. God wants us to value another's promotion over personal position. He wants us to cover the mistakes of others, showing mercy, not judgment. These are the essential issues that *really matter to God*! Again, remember that it is more important to be kind and humble than to prove your point—even though you may be right!

Every wise person I've ever known was also a quiet person. My father is a wise and meek man who rarely says much, but he has great power and discernment hidden beneath his silence. He has "power under control." Most of the godly people I know never like to talk about themselves. When they talk, they talk mostly about the things of the Lord, what God has done in their lives! The Bible says that when the Holy Spirit speaks, He always glorifies the Father and the Son. Humility does not speak of itself. Humility always glorifies the greater one. **Any person who has the genuine fruit of humility doesn't like to talk about him or herself in grand ways.**

"Let nothing be done through strife or vainglory; but in lowliness of mind let each esteem other as better than themselves" (Phil. 2:3). That means, "In lowliness I desire to put others above myself. In lowliness I am committed to love other people whether we agree on everything or not, working with them to get God's mission accomplished." When I do this, it always lifts my life to a new level of greatness. Acting independently as a god unto myself is not a part of His Kingdom. Striving to attain attention, or making decisions apart from God's purpose, are not a part of God's Kingdom. Others will always be a part of the choices you make, in order for you to learn how to minister to the needs of the Body. That husband or wife whom you live with becomes a "grace producer" for you. With two opinions in the house, one becomes the winner by honoring the other mate's desires more than his or her own. Esteem and honor others more than you honor yourself.

Test of Humility

Isaiah the prophet revealed the true test of humility and Jesus Christ demonstrated it in person. Jesus gave us the pattern for godly humility described in Isaiah 53. He was despised, rejected, a man of sorrows, acquainted with grief, stricken, smitten, afflicted, wounded for our transgressions, bruised for our iniquities, and stripped of peace for the sake of others. He was oppressed, and though He was afflicted, "yet He opened not His mouth" (Is. 53:7). In His humiliation, justice was taken from Him.

Jesus was denied justice, and though He had every right to call thousands of angels down from Heaven to destroy our race, though the ugliness of our sin on Him forced His Father to turn away and leave Him alone, He pressed Himself into death so you and I could have life. He literally esteemed our lives "better" than His own. That is true humility and true love. Even in the midst of injustice Jesus remained meek. Now God wants us to lay down our comforts and our privacies for the good of others as the Holy Spirit leads us.

If we are walking in humility we will not be offended by the actions of others. We will stay sweet!

This next point is extremely important. A true test of humility comes to us when we are denied justice. Can we say, "I am who I am by the grace of God. He is my source of strength and protection"? Every time we get challenged in any area of our lives, can we say, "I'm nothing anyway, but the greater One who lives in me makes me valuable and gives me dignity in His Kingdom"? Think about this every time you don't receive what you think you deserve. If it wasn't for Jesus, I'd be spending an eternity in hell. That's a pretty sobering word.

Let this mind be in you, which was also in Christ Jesus: who, being in the form of God, thought it not robbery to be equal with God: but made Himself of no reputation, and took upon Him the form of a servant, and was made in the likeness of men (Philippians 2:5-7).

Here Paul shows us what attitude we are supposed to have toward God and each other through the example of Jesus Christ. Jesus was God Almighty, but chose to become a slave or servant of the human race. It was this attitude of humility and trust that allowed Jesus to bring salvation to an independent, prideful, unbelieving world.

God has given us everything pertaining to life and godliness (see 2 Pet. 1:3). It is His gift, and we are nothing without it. That revelation is a great foundation for a life of fruitfulness in this faceless generation!

This beautiful poem by Mrs. B.V. Cornwall expresses how God desires us to be His humble servants and chosen vessels.

Chosen Vessel

The Master was searching for a vessel to use;
On the shelf there were many—which one would He choose?

"Take me," cried the gold one, "I'm shiny and bright,
I'm of great value and I do things just right.
My beauty and lustre will outshine the rest
And for Someone like You, Master, gold would be best!"

The Master passed on with no word at all;
He looked at a silver urn, narrow and tall;
"I'll serve You, dear Master, I'll pour out Your wine
And I'll be at Your table whenever You dine,
My lines are so graceful, my carvings so true,
And silver will always compliment You."

Unheeding the Master passed on to the brass.
It was widemouthed and shallow, and polished like glass.
"Here! Here!" cried the vessel, "I know I will do,
Place me on Your table for all men to view."

"Look at me," called the goblet of crystal so clear,
"My transparency shows my contents so dear,
Though fragile am I, I will serve You with pride,
And I'm sure I'll be happy in Your house to abide."

The Master came next to a vessel of wood,
Polished and carved, it solidly stood.
"You may use me, dear Master," the wooden bowl said,
"But I'd rather You used me for fruit, not for bread!"

Then the Master looked down and saw a vessel of clay,
Empty and broken it helplessly lay.
No hope had the vessel that the Master might choose,
To cleanse and make whole, to fill and to use.

"Ah! This is the vessel I've been hoping to find,
I will mend and use it and make it all Mine."

"I need not the vessel with pride of its self;
Nor the one who is narrow to sit on the shelf;

Nor one who is bigmouthed and shallow and loud;
Nor one who displays his contents so proud;
Nor the one who thinks he can do all things just right;
But this plain earthly vessel filled with My power and might."

Then gently He lifted the vessel of clay.
Mended and cleansed it and filled it that day.
Spoke to it kindly, "There's work you must do,
Just pour out to others as I pour into you."

Mrs. B.V. Cornwall
(Iverna Tompkins' mother)

Chapter 7

The Greatest Is the Child

Children possess an uncanny ability to cut to the core of the issue, to expose life to the bone, and strip away the barnacles that cling to the hull of our too sophisticated pseudo-civilization. One reason for this, I believe, is that children have not mastered our fine art of deception that we call "finesse." Another is that they are so "lately come from God" that faith and trust are second nature to them. They have not acquired the obstructions to faith that come with education; they possess instead unrefined wisdom, a gift from God. —Gloria Gaither

Whosoever therefore shall humble himself as this little child, the same is greatest in the kingdom of heaven (Matthew 18:4).

Childlike humility transforms our personal relationships and brings a completeness to our lives. Without this kind of humility we are headed for contention and strife. God designed us to live in interdependent relationships. We are to be "people people." Even more so, we are to be "little people people." We were created to thrive and prosper in rich, lifelong relationships with our families, our parents, our spouses, our extended family members, work associates, and the family of God. What stops us from living life the way God planned it? Three "s" words come to mind: sin, selfishness, and separation.

Loving, long-term relationships are essential to our health and personal fulfillment; they also are vitally important to God. We need joy, peace, and righteousness in our personal relationships because that is where the Kingdom of God is found.

Childlike Humility Receives Correction

My son, despise not the chastening of the Lord; neither be weary of His correction: for whom the Lord loveth, He correcteth; even as a father the son in whom he delighteth (Proverbs 3:11-12).

If the Lord is correcting you, it is because He wants to create something of great significance out of your life. For most of us, the Lord's correction will be a daily experience. If we desire to grow and are asking God for His purposes to be done in our lives, we will need to change. That change requires a childlike humility, knowing that "God's ways are not our ways and His thoughts are not our thoughts" (see Is. 55:8).

Do you see why meekness and childlike humility are so important to God? As we mentioned earlier, the Bible says that we cannot even receive the Word of God without meekness: "And receive with meekness the engrafted word, which is able to save your souls" (Jas. 1:21b). If we can't receive correction ourselves, then we can't expect anybody around us to receive it! Are you having trouble with your children or your job? Are you noticing trouble spots in your life where it seems nobody is receiving your correction? Check yourself—are you receiving correction from God? This may be a difficult lesson to learn, but our success in life is directly related to how well we receive correction. Remember, when the Lord is correcting us, that means He loves us.

God wants us to become like little children who know they need guidance and who have an unending appetite for love and affection. Children want to be corrected. It brings them security. When we become like children in humility, God will guide us. Jesus didn't leave any room for debate on this issue. He bluntly confronted His bickering disciples in an unforgettable way:

> *At the same time came the disciples unto Jesus, saying, Who is the greatest in the kingdom of heaven? And Jesus called a little child unto Him, and set him in the midst of them, and said, Verily I say unto you, Except ye be converted, and become as little children, ye shall not enter into the kingdom of heaven. Whosoever therefore shall humble himself as this little child, the same is greatest in the kingdom of heaven. And whoso shall receive one such little child in My name receiveth Me. But whoso shall offend one of these little ones which believe in Me, it were better for him that a millstone were hanged about his neck, and that he were drowned in the depth of the sea* (Matthew 18:1-6).

Little children are very teachable. They quickly receive instruction from trusted adults and parents. Children aren't offended when their parents gently correct them for wrongdoing or instruct them toward a better path. Many times we take God's correction as a personal insult and become offended. God only wants to move us into deeper waters of maturity, responsibility, and greatness. He wants to grant us every single desire of our heart, but He abides by His own law of sowing and reaping. If we have sowed something improper, He'll bring correction so we can sow the right seeds and achieve the desire we've been longing for.

My husband is a very wise man with a deep knowledge and reverence for the Word of God. Many times, God uses Tom to bring instruction and correction into my life. I could murmur in my pride and say, "Who does he think he is? What does he think he is doing?" But I don't get offended because these words flood my mind and heart: "The wise in heart will receive commandments" (Prov. 10:8a).

A fool will rebel, but a godly man or woman will humbly listen and thank the Lord. God begins with gentle nudgings and gradually gets firmer in His correction if we fail to receive it. First the Holy Spirit will speak gently to our hearts through God's Word. If we recoil, get mad, and try to pass off that word to someone else, He will send the same message in a stronger form. Eventually, if God's "kind messenger" is ignored, then for the sake of your heart cry to God, He will send a "cruel messenger" to get your attention in an unavoidable way. No person, wise or otherwise, wants to be in that position! The pure heart yearns for godly instruction.

Humility is pure. In other words, if you have trouble receiving correction or guidance, then analyze your heart and ask God to heal and cleanse away the unseen hurts, wounds, and scars inside you. Feelings of rejection or intimidation could be hindering your progress in purity. God doesn't want to condemn you; He wants to heal you and teach you how to move closer to Him. Don't be surprised if He takes you to "humility school."

Childlike Humility Produces Honesty

Childlike humility goes hand in hand with honesty. When we are humble like a little child we have very little to hide. If we are clinging to pride and selfishness, then there is little that we want to reveal. Little children are *painfully* honest, for the most part. They typically "tell it all."

My little daughter was in a nearby room one day while I was taking a bath. When the phone rang, Laurelle quickly ran to answer it. She said, "Hello, this is Laurelle..." (I was expecting a phone call for an interview with a national radio program at the time). My daughter didn't know it, but I had quietly picked up the phone in another room to say hello. I overheard her say, "Uh, Mommy can't come to the phone right now, she's in the bathtub naked!" (I nearly choked with laughter!) That's my daughter! She tells it all! It was just hilarious. The man on the other end of the line was so embarrassed that he didn't know what to say! Finally I regained control of myself and spoke up, "Hi, Mr. So-and-So. That was my little girl. Don't they just tell it all?!" I talked frankly about it with him and before long he was laughing too. I was glad I didn't have one of those TV phones!

Children are basically honest. They generally don't hide or camouflage things (until they are taught to do it). Humble people have retained this same innocent honesty because it is the basis for true humility. We can only be genuine when we understand and admit our weaknesses as well as our strengths. Humble people are honest about their gifts. Their self-esteem does not come from their talented performance. Although they are confident in their gifts, their self-esteem does not come from the gifts, but from knowing God's unconditional love and acceptance of them as a person!

There is a big difference between being childish and childlike. The *childish* person always wants something. This person's life is a big "I want" that just keeps growing. It's like the bottomless pit that is never full. A *childlike* person receives the grace of God *as God gives it* with thanksgiving, not complaining. We need to receive the blessings of God meekly, recognizing that His gifts are given freely. They are not a measure of our value to Him or to the Body of Christ; they are a measure of His bounty. You are loved by God because you are special and you are His pleasure. It is that

101

simple. The Bible says that the Christians in the first century Church were "breaking bread from house to house, [eating] their meat with gladness and singleness of heart" (Acts 2:46). They knew how to be contented with God's provision of fellowship and joy.

Childlike Humility Is Interdependent, Not Codependent

Deep in our hearts, we all want relationships more than material blessings. The most passionate desire anyone has is for someone to be willing to lay down his life for him or her (see Jn. 15:13). We each want deep, intimate, trusting relationships with God and with other people who love and value us. Children need the influence of others to grow up. **Humility helps us walk in relationship with God and other people.** It fosters a healthy and holy interdependence between members of the Body of Christ, since we all need the gifts and strengths God has planted in our brothers and sisters.

Now there are diversities of gifts, but the same Spirit. And there are differences of administrations, but the same Lord. And there are diversities of operations, but it is the same God which worketh all in all. But the manifestation of the Spirit is given to every man to profit withal (1 Corinthians 12:4-7).

Your problem may not be lack of humility. You may be hindered by insecurity, low self-esteem, or severe codependency to others. If this describes your situation, you need to realize that *God has given you something that will bless others,* and they've been given something that will bless you. You may be too dependent on somebody else's strength, saying in your heart, "I'm not good at anything. I'm going to have fellowship with somebody else because that person is smart and successful." That is codependency, not humility. God wants you to live an abundant life with fulfillment and joy in *Him.* He made you to be above and not beneath, for you are unique and special to Him. He wants you to bless others with your gifts.

God is the great leveler in the Church. He takes the valleys (the insecure and codependent) and builds them up. He takes the mountains (the overconfident and independent) and "shaves them off" to make one smooth highway through the wilderness from His throne to the earth. The highway of holiness, in Christ, will reach our fallen generation. He wants every one of us to take our place and keep our eyes on *Him*, not on our strengths or our weaknesses! He will supply all that we need. In every situation, He measures us according to our hearts, not our outward appearance or abilities.

I'm grateful that I can sing and speak, but I'm fully aware that these are not only gifts, they are also great responsibilities. I stand before God in a "holy fear and trembling" that I will be faithful to use His gifts for His glory and purpose. I am certain it is His anointing that creates a passion within others, not my abilities. My words are only dead letters without Him breathing His life upon them. In addition to that, God will hold me accountable for every idle, opinionated word I speak.

Two men went up into the temple to pray; the one a Pharisee, and the other a publican. The Pharisee stood and prayed thus with himself, God, I thank Thee, that I am not as other men are, extortioners, unjust, adulterers, or even as this publican. I fast twice in the week, I give tithes of all that I possess. And the publican, standing afar off, would not lift up so much as his eyes unto heaven, but smote upon his breast, saying, God be merciful to me a sinner. I tell you, this man went down to his house justified rather than the other: for every one that exalteth himself shall be abased; and he that humbleth himself shall be exalted (Luke 18:10-14).

What exalts us in the sight of God is humility. As we admit our mistakes before God, He will lift us up and strengthen us where we are weak. This is letting His strength be perfected in our weakness. This is a true demonstration of childlike humility and trust.

Childlike Humility Has No Limits

But the fruit of the Spirit is love, joy, peace, longsuffering, gentleness, goodness, faith, meekness, temperance: against such there is no law (Galatians 5:22-23).

There is no limit or law to how much we can grow in God. Ask God to strengthen the weak areas of your life. That's the way of a child. At one point in her life, my daughter thought I knew everything. When she had a question, she would come to me, take my hand, and say, "Mommy, how do you know about that? See, Mommy? You know everything. I think you are really smart!" I just looked in her little face and said, "Little Honey, if you only knew how much I really don't know! The smartest one is Jesus, and we're all trying to follow Him. He's the smartest one of all. As long as we listen to Him, we'll be all right!"

Humble people are obedient people who never get set in their ways. God intends to conform you to the image of Jesus (see Rom. 8:29). Some of us have farther to go than others, but whatever you do, don't compare yourself with other people. It is unwise to compare ourselves with others. We must all look to Jesus as our example of humility and servanthood.

If we try to be someone else, we'll always be second place. Do you remember Simeon and Anna in the Bible? They weren't widely acclaimed or made popular. What made them great? They were childlike, they were humble, and they were absolutely obedient to the call of God even though no one noticed them most of their lives. We tend, as we get older, to get set in our ways. Notice that those were older people who just kept on listening. They didn't shut down—or retire. They refired!

God has an established order in His Kingdom. Where His order is violated, there is chaos. Disorder can wreck our life, our family, our church, or our ministry. God preserves order through the virtue of humility in our lives. The Bible tells us to "obey them that have the rule" over us in the Lord, as well as the magistrates and governors in the land (Heb. 13:17; see also Tit. 3:1). God wants us to be humble and obedient, even if it hurts. We can fulfill our destiny only when we submit to the will of God in honoring spiritual authority. There are no limits to the degree of greatness that young people can walk in. They simply need to honor and respect natural and spiritual eldership. God has prepared some respecting and respectable young men and women for leadership today.

Childlike Humility Is Forgiving

Finally, childlike disciples of Christ don't lash out in judgment. Little children are so forgiving that even if their mommy or daddy hurts them, they will come running back into their parent's arms. **To be childlike, to be humble, is to be forgiving.** A humble person is always looking inside to check his or her heart. Such a person wants to respond to others correctly. When we respond to others correctly, God is quick to answer our prayers! If we walk in love and humility, and are quick to respond in forgiveness, God says He will do anything that you ask according to His will (see 1 Jn. 5:14-15). But first and foremost, He says we are to forgive. Humility will always win. It always comes out on top.

Chapter 8

Humble Trust

The highest level of faith is trust because it goes beyond our own understanding.

Faith Is Humble Trust

Jesus quoted from Micah 6:8, which named the three "weightier matters" of the law:

Woe unto you, scribes and Pharisees, hypocrites! for ye pay tithe of mint and anise and cummin, and have omitted the weightier matters of the law, judgment, mercy, and faith: these ought ye to have done, and not to leave the other undone. Ye blind guides, which strain at a gnat, and swallow a camel (Matthew 23:23-24).

Jesus carefully linked His Father's ancient requirements for greatness named by Micah the prophet with the most important issues in life: judgment (or justice), mercy, and faith toward God.

He hath shewed thee, O man, what is good; and what doth the Lord require of thee, but to do justly, and to love mercy, and to walk humbly with thy God? (Micah 6:8)

Although Micah says humility is a requirement for greatness, Jesus substituted the corresponding and parallel virtue of faith in His rebuke in Matthew chapter 23. Humility and faith are directly related to one another.

You may ask, "How do they correspond?" The highest level of faith is trust. Trust requires great humility because it requires you to believe God's promises when you have no human understanding of *how* God will accomplish His promise.

Trust Is Humble

There is a story told of a young girl who went for a walk with her father in a dark forest. Hand in hand they walked together, but in the midst of the deepest dark woods the father purposely let go of the girl's hand. Desperately she began to search for his hand, crying out to find him. Then all at once the father stepped in front of the girl and she grabbed hold of her daddy. As soon as she did, she said, "Oh, Daddy, I'm so glad I found you!"

After every promise has been rehearsed and you've searched desperately for God's hand in your life with no avail, always remember, you can trust God's heart. Proverbs 3:5-8 says:

Trust in the Lord with all thine heart; and lean not unto thine own understanding. In all thy ways acknowledge Him, and He shall direct thy paths. Be not wise in thine own eyes: fear the Lord, and depart from evil. It shall be health to thy navel, and marrow to thy bones.

God teaches us how to trust Him in all things. That is what pleases God. Humble trust is demonstrated by an obedience to God's Word before having a revelation of it. In the middle of trials and temptations, trust will obey God without needing all the answers. When I was growing up I would ask my father the why question. Sometimes he would just say, "It's because of the *fratasis*." It was just a word he used to mean, "I don't really know why, so just accept the situation as it is." This taught me to trust more. It showed me I didn't need to have all the questions answered to believe God's heart. I just trusted Him and if He chose to explain the why, then that was up to Him.

It should go without saying that God is trustworthy. He not only has our best interests in mind, but He has proven it through His loving acts of mercy and sacrifice throughout history! No one can really obey the commands of God unless they cross the great hurdle of trust. I am convinced that much of what happens to us that we do not understand occurs because God just wants to bring us home safely. Be prepared for miracles when you pray, "Order my steps in your Word, O Lord, and let no sin have dominion over me" (see Ps. 119:133).

God has designed us to believe His Word, to honor it, to quote it, and to live it. When we pray and believe His Word, He has promised to perform it. We have the responsibility to know and understand what God's Word says about our lives. What happens when we can't hear what God is saying specifically about our situation or our problem? What happens when all the Scriptures we have prayed over and truly believed aren't producing results? That's when we trust. We never stop believing God's Word and what He promised. We recognize that He is faithful to His promise, but in the meantime what is being developed in us is a greater good—faith and patience. It's wonderful to see immediate answers to prayers and instant miracles when we believe. But perhaps it takes a greater faith to put your faith in the Lord and trust Him when you don't understand His ways. It should give us great peace to know that we don't have to be in control. God is in control.

Our God is jealous for our attention and affection. I believe He gradually removes things in our lives that keep us from totally loving and trusting Him. In Jeremiah 18:4 the Lord told Jeremiah, "And the vessel that he made of clay was marred in the hand of the potter: so he made it again another vessel, as seemed good to the potter to make it."

Our biggest struggle is when God makes another vessel and He uses the hammer of His Word or the fire of His Spirit. The molding process can hurt! Our natural mind says, "If God really loved me, He would bless me." Then I read in His Word, "As many as I love, I rebuke and chasten" (Rev. 3:19a). God knows what love really is. It's not merely a feeling. God's love toward us provokes us to change to become more like Him. God's love chastens us in order to make the insignificant into the important, the irrelevant into true reality, the nobodies and the nothings into great big somebodies and somethings. When we truly become the vessel that God has chosen us to be, it won't really matter what we have.

Many of Christ's followers never advance to the greatness of their calling because they look for the immediate blessing of faith rather than trusting God when He is silent. God is as faithful in His silence as He is when He is talking. Those silent times teach us the depth of faith, which is trust.

God says, "For I know the thoughts that I think toward you, saith the Lord, thoughts of peace, and not of evil, to give you an expected end" (Jer. 29:11).

God has perfect and gracious intentions for us. No matter what He asks or commands us to do, when we trust Him it is not difficult to obey because we know that "Father knows best."

God Reasons With Us

God builds basic trust in us as He patiently deals with our imperfections. He even *models* everything He wants to see established in us! He teaches us gentleness and tolerance by patiently working with our inconsistencies. Jesus gave His own life for us out of pure love and gave us the supreme example of giving. He also teaches us grace by mercifully making allowances for our strong wills until we can trust His Word of simplicity:

Come now, and let us reason together, saith the Lord: though your sins be as scarlet, they shall be as white as snow; though they be red like crimson, they shall be as wool. If ye be willing and obedient, ye shall eat the good of the land (Isaiah 1:18-19).

In the initial stages of building trust, a little child will ask many questions. God patiently explains many things to us, and He even condescends to graciously reason with us—creatures whose intellect isn't remotely on par with His, and whose questions are nearly always tainted with self-interest, excuses, or impure motives. "What is man, that Thou shouldest magnify him? and that Thou shouldest set Thine heart upon him?" (Job 7:17) God's desire is to reveal Himself to us so clearly that we know His character and are sure His intentions for us are good, in order that we will instantly and joyfully trust and obey Him exactly as Jesus did.

As we learn about trust, our heavenly Father reveals His forbearance toward us by allowing us a certain amount of liberty to err in order to show us how to minister grace to others. Some people find it harder to trust than others because their natural wills and fleshly tendencies are stronger and more obvious. God gains their trust by meeting them at their level.

God Exemplifies Trust

An example can be the best teacher for some of us. God's abundant tolerance for human weaknesses establishes a rich foundation of trust that is described in the Book of First Peter:

Feed the flock of God which is among you, taking the oversight thereof, not by constraint, but willingly; not for

111

filthy lucre, but of a ready mind; neither as being lords over God's heritage, but being ensamples to the flock. And when the chief Shepherd shall appear, ye shall receive a crown of glory that fadeth not away (1 Peter 5:2-4).

Teachers and ministers who are wise enough to balance the need to guide and instruct with tolerance and understanding are able to minimize fear and condemnation in those they lead. On the other hand, those who put a heavy emphasis on concepts of "headship" and "rule" could be more concerned with corporate management than with personal leadership. They may emphasize headship at the cost of personal growth and loving relationships. This can produce fear and misunderstanding in those they lead.

Herein is our love made perfect, that we may have boldness in the day of judgment: because as He is, so are we in this world. There is no fear in love; but perfect love casteth out fear: because fear hath torment. He that feareth is not made perfect in love. We love Him, because He first loved us (1 John 4:17-19).

Fear and torment thrive when people must live under the threat of heavy punishment. God, however, wants us not to fear but to trust Him. Greater trust in a relationship produces greater submission in a relationship.

Choose to Trust God

"Can two walk together, except they be agreed?" (Amos 3:3) **It takes trust and a willingness for us to humbly walk with God.** The Lord purposely describes us as His children and Himself as our Father, for that is the clearest image of the relationship He has desired from the beginning. Just as Adam and Eve walked with God in the cool of the day, our Father God longs to walk with us every day of our lives. After all, children hold their parents' hands because they trust the parents, and the parents make them feel loved, valued, and secure. **Trust is the deepest form of faith because it goes beyond our own understanding.** When we trust God, our lives reflect a humble and single-minded walk through life based on the simple fact that *nothing* can separate us from the love of our God.

> *Who shall separate us from the love of Christ? shall tribu-*
> *lation, or distress, or persecution, or famine, or nakedness,*
> *or peril, or sword? ... Nay, in all these things we are more*
> *than conquerors through Him that loved us. For I am*
> *persuaded, that neither death, nor life, nor angels, nor*
> *principalities, nor powers, nor things present, nor things to*
> *come, nor height, nor depth, nor any other creature, shall*
> *be able to separate us from the love of God, which is in*
> *Christ Jesus our Lord* (Romans 8:35,37-39).

Trust is expressed when you make choices that are contrary to your human will or thought, and when you choose to follow the values of God instead of human reasoning. Every time you choose to believe God instead of circumstances, and every time you stand on your belief that God has a destiny for you no matter how long it takes to fulfill it, you are demonstrating *humble trust.* God is blessed when you choose to believe that you are what God says you are! You are powerful, not pitiful. You are loved, not lacking. You are received, not rejected!

Throughout my singing ministry, I've had opportunities to be with some very well known ministers, both in public meetings and on television. As I was thanking God one day for these "open doors" and the "big breaks" He had blessed me with, He said to me, "What most people look for is a 'big break.' What I look for is a 'big breaking.' " Before God can make us great, He must break us great. Our real "big break" is God's purifying, purging, humbling work deep within our hearts, removing all selfish desires, enabling us to trust totally in His ability to provide for us.

Our trust in God's plan for life is not synonymous with a great name or popularity. Greatness does not mean getting a big mailing list so everyone can send you their "seed-offering." Some of the greatest ministers I know today are those who are doing what they can to love and support their pastor and the people in their own local church. They are going out on their days off to help build the Kingdom of God in their own community. Kingdom greatness requires this attitude of humility that is faithful to serve the people right in the place where God has planted us. It means *forgiving* the hurts and *forgetting* the betrayals we receive from the ones we serve and pray for on a day-to-day basis.

This humble trust might even mean accepting the blame for things you have not done. It surely means being the example of love and forgiveness to the wagging tongues caught up in judgment and accusation around you. Remember Paul's instruction to Timothy when he said, "And *the servant of the Lord* must not strive; but be gentle unto all men, apt to teach, patient, in meekness instructing those that oppose themselves; if God peradventure will give them repentance to the acknowledging of the truth" (2 Tim. 2:24-25). A great servant of the Lord will not fight with others so that he can lead and instruct others in the way of humility.

With an attitude of humble trust, our churches, ministries, families, and organizations will be blessed with the sensitivity and warmth that make them places of hope for people, places they will want to belong to. People naturally respond to an atmosphere and an attitude of servanthood. It is God's unconditional love in action, lived out in human flesh. With an attitude of this servanthood-type love and care for others, we will never fail to overcome and achieve Kingdom greatness. Servant-love will always be victorious because it never seeks its own. It is not touchy or resentful. We are truly great servants of God, humbly trusting Him, when we can serve others without being offended. This is the sign of real maturity and Christian character. James likens this person to a perfect man who is able to bridle his tongue no matter what happens to him (see Jas. 3:2).

Developing Trusting Relationships

How do we build trusting relationships? What helps trust to flourish and grow? Since trust is a foundation in relationships, here are a few facts that help us develop trust.

1. *Trust grows when we stay faithful to our promises to others.* God has given us His Word, and He has never failed to honor it. He commands us to follow His example and "swear to our own hurt and change not" (see Ps. 15:4). He wants us to keep our given word as diligently as He does, and God "hastens over it to perform it" (see Jer. 1:12).

2. *Trust thrives in the presence of joy.* God rejoices over us with singing (see Zeph. 3:17). God is a fun God. He actually likes to play with us! He enjoys life because He created it. He literally created us to be His pleasure (see Rev. 4:11). He loves being with us. Our trust in God deepens as we see His rich sense of humor, as well as His infinite ability to enjoy us in all our comic faults! When we see how relaxed God is on His throne, then we can relax and trust that life is good. Knowing that God loves us and is in control of our lives increases our trust.

3. *Trust grows as we share intimate times together.* God says, "Be still, and know that I am God..." (Ps. 46:10). The most precious moment in life is when God speaks to us personally. Insecure people always feel compelled to be busy or to talk when there is a lull in a conversation. God wants us to wait on Him, to hear His voice, and to know Him better

through those times of intimacy. He wants us to know He is with us through every situation. This depth of relationship requires trust. Though we cannot see Him, yet we believe Him.

Trust in our relationships with others often grows best through nonverbal communication. God's Word tells us that "deep calleth unto deep," reflecting the nature of the spirit man alive in each of us (Ps. 42:7). If you have a deep relationship with someone, you can spend more time with him or her in utter silence because you are at peace in each other's love.

4. *Trust grows as we realize that God is sensitive and has feelings too.* God demonstrated His infinite trustworthiness through the greatest love letter ever written. His footprints in the dusty roads of Israel and the bloody trail up the Via Dolorosa and beneath the tree of Calvary openly declare God's unequalled love for our fallen race!

The events of the cross reveal God's very heart to us! His sacrifice and victory at Calvary supernaturally increase our ability to trust God because that event forever transforms God from "a bunch of facts in a history book of old do's and don'ts" into a love story filled with unequalled self-sacrifice and unrequited love. God revealed His heart and feelings directly to our spirits because He is Spirit and because He can relate to us more powerfully in the realm of the spirit and the heart. This relationship allows us to trust Him more fully. Since we are emotional beings, God emotes with us. Trust grows when we understand that our great big God has feelings too.

5. *Trust grows as we learn to understand God's way of thinking.* God does nothing through force or compulsion. We are not puppets on a string because God gave us the

right of choice. We are loved, accepted, and even encouraged to become great in God's eyes—even if we blow it royally and repeatedly! God is committed to our personal growth. He wants us to understand Him! He believes in us.

We achieve the highest level of trust in our interpersonal relationships when we genuinely want the other person to become everything he or she can be. As we let go of our personal agendas and learn more about God's plan, we will find our trust level growing. At the opposite extreme, spiritual paralysis occurs when we try to control our relationship with God or others through deception or hidden agendas. When we learn to accept and trust God's way of thinking for our lives, obedience to His will follows.

The most beautiful example of this can be experienced in the marriage covenant. It is the miracle of two people choosing to believe in and love one another—despite their flaws and failures. It is no wonder that God likens His relationship with the Church to the human marriage covenant! Only trust can make it last!

Three Characteristics of Trust

You know you're trusting God if these three characteristics are evident in you life.

The first characteristic of trust is obedience. A beautiful example of obedient trust is seen in the life of St. Francis of Assisi. During a difficult time in his life he went to visit the Pope to discuss the persecution he endured due to his popularity and beliefs. The Pope, not impressed with his appearance of rags because of his oath of poverty, told St. Francis to "go roll in the mud with the pigs."

In obedience to the Pope St. Francis went out and did just exactly as he said, then returned to speak with him. The Pope was so impressed with his humble obedience that great favor was bestowed on him from that day forward. The whole Franciscan order that exists today is a result of one man's humble obedience.

Obedience is a characteristic of trust. St. Francis was not trusting in a man when he obeyed the command to roll in the mud. He was humbling himself to the higher law of God's Kingdom. He knew God honors submission and obedience to those in authority. No matter how corrupt that authority may be, when you put your trust in God's order and obey God's delegated authority, you are really obeying God. When you obey God, He covers you and defends you.

When there is a genuine love that exists in a relationship, obedient submission is much easier. We desire to serve those we love. When we obey at the times when it is risky, true trust is demonstrated.

When Gad came to David in the cave of Adullam, David was comfortable and safe there. But, "the prophet Gad said unto David, Abide not in the hold; depart, and get thee into the land of Judah" (1 Sam. 22:5a). Adullam was a stronghold, which is a place where water was in abundance and food was stored. It was also a secure military base. When we are in our own secure place of abundance, provision, and protection, then it is hard to move on to another place. God will often require us to move out of the comfort zone to a discomfort zone in order to develop trust in our character.

If you ask God to make you into a great leader or minister, be prepared to do some things you may not understand in obedience to the Word of God. When God asks us (like He did Peter) to step out of the boat and walk on the water, He is just teaching us to trust Him. "Some trust in chariots, and some in horses: but we will remember the name of the Lord our God" (Ps. 20:7).

Comfortable Christian living and trusting in the ways of man do not produce the God-kind of faith. When things get a bit uncomfortable as a Christian, just know that God is working some greatness in your life. He's teaching you to trust Him above your own abilities, strengths, and provisions. He wants us to know that He is all you really need. He is enough! God will lead you into victory.

The second characteristic of trust is joy. This means that no matter what circumstances look like, if you're trusting God, you have an inner joy because you know God is your provider, protector, peacemaker, and the possessor of your life.

Although the fig tree shall not blossom, neither shall fruit be in the vines; the labour of the olive shall fail, and the fields shall yield no meat; the flock shall be cut off from the fold, and there shall be no herd in the stalls: yet I will rejoice in the Lord, I will joy in the God of my salvation (Habakkuk 3:17-18).

When everything in life seems like it's falling and failing, the one who trusts in God can laugh. Joy and peace are evidences that the Kingdom of God is ruling in our lives. Christian joy doesn't have its roots in success or failure, abundance or lack, good times or bad. Joy springs up in our hearts because it knows the salvation and deliverance that come from God. In fact, in Philemon 7 the word for joy has its roots in *charis*, the Greek word for "grace." That is the unmerited, undeserved favor and love of God. When we trust that God loves and accepts us just as we are because of grace, we possess true inner joy. The apostle Paul prayed, "Now the God of hope fill you with all joy and peace in believing" (Rom. 15:13a).

One of the greatest gifts God has given my husband and me is the blessing of a daughter named Laurelle. I have a tendency to be such a progressive visionary that God has used her to help me slow down and enjoy the simple things in life. Through various circumstances I learned how to laugh at myself, laugh at the devil, and most of all to laugh with God. Psalm 2:4a says, "He that sitteth in the heavens shall laugh."

For the kingdom of God is not meat and drink; but righteousness, and peace, and joy in the Holy Ghost (Romans 14:17).

When we are really trusting God and living in His Kingdom, we are filled with joy. People and circumstances can take away everything we've got, but no one or nothing can take our joy! Things can discourage us, confuse us, and even disappoint us, but His joy remains. The next time you feel like a failure, remember that Jesus is always smiling on you, even when you fail.

The Bible says, "Blessed is the people that know *the joyful sound*: they shall walk, O Lord, in the light of Thy countenance" (Ps. 89:15). It is important that you hear yourself laugh and give praise to God. When you hear it, even if it is forced, it will bring strength to your inner man. When your inner man hears the sound of joy and laughter, it is like a healing, restoring medicine to your body and soul. That is why God says, "A merry heart doeth good like a medicine: but a broken spirit drieth the bones" (Prov. 17:22).

Trust has an ability to laugh with God. Trust has the ability to look at the final page of life's book and see that we win! Let your faith explode with hope in God's plan for your life and enjoy the ride! Obey God's sabbath and relax a bit. Appreciate the little things in life. Do more reflecting on life and what's really important. Really, the little things in life mean so very much! Find ways to stimulate both your spiritual senses and your natural senses. Take care of your spirit, your mind, and your body. Do some things in life that are worth remembering. Take your kids to the park or buy your wife a rose. Cook your husband a candlelight dinner. By all means don't be so worried about everything! Take your responsibilities serious, but not yourself. Remember the characteristic of trust is joy. Rejoice! God has things under control.

God is laughing at His enemies, so why aren't you? Come on, get out of the rut and split a gut! God is on your side. Don't argue with your enemies. Jesus said "to agree with your enemies quickly" and let God handle them (see Mt. 5:25). You have more important things to do than to wear a depressed-looking face around other people! There is no greater evidence of trust than to just haul off and laugh when the devil does something. He's been defeated, while we are more than conquerors and bound for gloryland! "The Lord is my strength and song, and is become my salvation" (Ps. 118:14).

The third characteristic of trust is fruitfulness. Jesus looked at the fig tree and cursed it from the roots up because it was barren. He said, "Every tree that bringeth not forth good fruit is hewn down, and cast into the fire. Wherefore by their fruits ye shall know them" (Mt. 7:19-20).

[handwritten marginal note: ? wasn't time to produce fruit! am confused. you too?]

Jesus didn't say that we would know them by their works. He said we would know them by their fruit. That's because you can counterfeit the works, but you can't counterfeit the fruit. Fruit is a result of what our trust is rooted in. It is a result of our attitude toward God.

But the fruit of the Spirit is love, joy, peace, longsuffering, gentleness, goodness, faith, meekness, temperance... (Galatians 5:22-23).

Fruitfulness is characterized by our commitments: commitments to our families, to our local church, and to God. Some Christians are floatful instead of faithful. That means rather than staying in one place with the same people and bearing fruit, they float from place to place living off the fruits of others. God calls this type of wandering spirit a curse. Such people look at life somewhat like a lottery. If they could just find the perfect church, the perfect mate, the perfect job, or the perfect friends, they will be fruitful.

Life is not a lottery. Life is a garden in which whatever we plant and tend bears fruit. God says in Psalm 92:13, "Those that be *planted* in the house of the Lord shall flourish in the courts of our God." The only real way to bear lasting fruit is to plant yourself and let God allow you to bloom where you are planted. It matters not what kind of soil God plants you in. If you trust Him for your growth and for giving you His wisdom and power, you can bear fruit in any soil.

One of the highest desires or dreams that I have ever personally possessed was to be involved in a large drama production. When a very large opportunity came my way and I was asked to be involved in a Broadway play, only then did I fully realize the importance of right values and priorities in life. I recognized more fully the values of God's Church family and His ministry in this earth. I realized more fully that we are not here on this earth to get a pat on the back. I realized more fully that my faithfulness to God's commitments is what will be judged in the final analysis of my life. For me to become involved in something as big as that would have taken me away from my priorities. But it's interesting to note that it took the refusal of a long-desired offer to help me realize what God deems most important: faithfulness to our covenants.

Fruitfulness has its foundation in trust. That's the reason God emphasizes to parents the need to train up their children in the way that they should go—when they are old they will not depart from it (see Prov. 22:6). As parents we do our children a great injustice if we do not sow into their lives what they need to bear fruit for tomorrow.

And such as do wickedly against the covenant shall he corrupt by flatteries: but the people that do know their God shall be strong, and do exploits (Daniel 11:32).

Knowing God is the only way to really trust Him. Take some time, even right now, and get to know Him. Do you want to progress toward knowing the greatness of God? Put everything aside for awhile and get alone with the Greatest One. Let His Spirit rub off on you. Let Him change you. It's what you've been waiting for. It's the thing you've been searching for. It's what really matters.

Chapter 9

Faith Toward God

We don't need "great big faith" in God; we need faith in a "great big God."

True Bible faith in God is one of the greatest acts of humility we can demonstrate before God. That is why God says that "without *faith* it is impossible to please Him" (Heb. 11:6). Faith is not simply knowing that God is able; it's the belief that He is willing! To walk in the faith that God will do what He said requires great humility and trust.

Corrie ten Boom once said, "Faith sees the impossible, believes the unbelievable, and receives the impossible." It's true, we are living in a day of miracles. I know there has never been a power shortage in Heaven, nor will there ever be. If we are lacking power in any area of our lives, we must ask God, "Where is our faith lacking? Where are we not trusting You, Lord?"

As we noted in the previous chapter, Jesus quoted from the Book of Micah about what the Lord requires of us (see Mic. 6:8). He refers to these requirements in Matthew 23:23 as the "weightier matters of the law." Jesus used the word *faith* in place of or as a synonym for Micah's phrase, "walking humbly with God."

The Greek word translated as "faith" in Matthew 23:23 is *pistus*, and it means "assurance and confidence, conviction." It is also rooted in the verb *pathos* or *pitho*, which means "to agree, to obey and to yield to authority." That is the root of the word for faith. We can see that Jesus was making a divine correlation between faith, obedience, and humility. The three are inseparable.

Faith During the Storm

Having faith toward God not only means believing God exists, but also receiving what God says concerning our lives. I believe our prayer life, our attitude, and our obedience to God are influenced by how we see Him. If we see God through our own ideas, experiences, and feelings, then our faith will be shipwrecked before it ever launches from shore.

Faith toward God comes as we acknowledge only what He says in His Word. It can be very humbling to think and feel one way about something, only to have God point out that it's not really that way at all!

Jesus' disciples were given instructions by Him to cross over the Sea of Galilee one day. After starting across, Jesus, tired from the day's busy tasks, took a nap in the back of the boat. Suddenly, a great storm came upon them and the boat was in danger of sinking. The disciples neither considered the words Jesus said about going to the other side or remembered who was in the boat with them.

If knowing what God has said about our situation isn't enough, He has also given us His very Spirit to dwell in us. The presence of the Godhead—Father, Son and Holy Spirit—live in our boat! God gave us His Word and the authority to use His name, and then He took up residence inside us as a guarantee for victory. The only

124

thing remaining in the equation is for us to believe that all the things He said about us are true!

In fear of the terrible storm that faced them, the disciples cried out, "Master, carest Thou not that we perish?" (Mk. 4:38b) Everything was great while Jesus was doing miracles and feeding everyone, but what about during the storm? So Jesus woke up and calmed the wind and the waves. Then He turned to His disciples and asked them, "Why are ye so fearful? how is it that ye have no faith?" (Mk. 4:40b)

It is one thing to believe while everything is going great; it is another to believe during the storms and adversities of life. Anyone can say "Amen!" when the evangelist is jumping through the hoops or juggling three translations of the Bible. Shouting "Hallelujah!" is easy when actions aren't required to prove what we believe. Sometimes Christians like to be heard *saying* all the right things, but God likes to see us *doing* all the right things. I say, "Let's leave the talking to those who've done the walking." In the meantime God asks us, "Where is your faith, big talker?"

As we humble ourselves and trust God during the times when things are tough we find our strength and ability to walk in victory growing. We also begin to develop faith to minister to the needs of others who are experiencing adversity. This is ultimately what God desires to work in us as His servants. Humility and faith toward God are demonstrated when we can reach out to the needs of others even in the middle of our own crisis.

I am reminded of the true story of Glenn Cunningham who, at the age of eight, was burned so badly from an exploding woodstove that the doctors said he probably wouldn't live. Determined he would go on with life, he overcame the pain and began to get better. The doctors then warned that even though he would live, they would have to take off both his legs because they were so badly burned. But Glenn refused to let them take his legs, determined that he would walk again.

He kept getting better and in six months he was healthy enough to get out of bed and walk on crutches. When he tried to walk, he could not feel his legs and fell down. Although those around him were very discouraged, Glenn told them not to worry because he would not only be able to walk some day, but he would even run. In fact, he told them he would even beat them in a race.

Every day Glenn worked on his legs, rubbing them, strengthening them until in six months he could actually take a few small steps. While everyone was surprised just to see him on his feet and felt sorry for him, Glenn was determined to be a great runner. Within two years Glenn was running.

By the time Glenn was 12, just four years after his accident, he was running races with high school-age kids and winning. Glenn continued to press on as a runner, training and exercising. He became such a good runner that he set a new record of 4 minutes, 24.7 seconds for the mile run. Glenn continued to improve his running, winning championships in many events in college. But the highlight came in 1933, when Glenn set a new U.S. and world record for the mile: 4 minutes, 6.7 seconds. He went on to be the greatest indoor mile runner of his day, winning more races than anyone else.

Glenn's accomplishments didn't end with his determination to be the best runner. Not only did he have 12 children of his own, but he made time and room to minister to young people in trouble and in need of help. Before he died in 1988, Glenn Cunningham ministered to more than 9,000 youth, helping them overcome their problems and get their lives back together.

When we stay determined to use the faith and ability God has given us and not quit, we can rise to new levels of greatness in the Kingdom. Let's be all we can be in God and help others be all they can be.

Faith Humbles Itself

For I say, through the grace given unto me, to every man that is among you, not to think of himself more highly than he ought to think; but to think soberly, according as God hath dealt to every man the measure of faith (Romans 12:3).

When you relate to God in an attitude of humility, you can accurately judge yourself. Faith has dignity and confidence, and it provides you with a built-in ability to accurately see your strengths and weaknesses. The Spirit of God will help you look at yourself honestly, so you can say, "This is where I need to change." The truly "undignified people" are those who think they have the ability to do something when they don't. Such people inevitably make fools of themselves in front of others. Don't think of yourself more highly than you ought, but ask God to show you your strengths and your weaknesses.

Someone once said, "The definition of a leader is a person that people are following. If no one is following us, then we're just going for a walk." "Followership" is an excellent test of our gifts and callings. If no one is being influenced by our ministry, then that's a good sign it's not what God has called us to. On the other hand, if people are truly blessed by what we are doing, it's a good possibility God has gifted us in that area. Real humility is having the faith to admit both what we have been called to and what we haven't. It's acknowledging what gifts God has given us and what gifts He has given to someone else.

Watch how people respond to the ministry gifts you use. Are they receiving your ministry and giftings? If they are, then thank God for it. Walk humbly with God by saying, "Okay, Lord, these are my strengths and these are my weaknesses. I give You the glory for every good thing that is within me, and for covering my weaknesses with Your glory!" We need to walk out this life together and work through the hard things as a spiritual family. Where one is weak, the other members of the Body should gather round and uplift and encourage that person.

For as we have many members in one body, and all members have not the same office: so we, being many, are one body in Christ, and every one members one of another (Romans 12:4-5).

The wide variety of God's gifts are distributed throughout the Body, so we all need one another. The person who thinks he can do everything by himself, the "Lone Ranger" believer, eventually discovers an area of lack where he needs someone else. The problem is, he may not know how to ask for or receive someone else's help! That is why we need one another—whether we are humble enough to admit it or not. The Lord's exhortation to think soberly about ourselves is also an exhortation for us to acknowledge our need for one another. He designed His Church to work together as a united body.

Faith Goes on With God

"Faith toward God" knows that it has not yet arrived at maturity. Rather, it presses forward, believing that it is moving toward the goal and toward God's high call!

But what things were gain to me, those I counted loss for Christ. Yea doubtless, and I count all things but loss for the excellency of the knowledge of Christ Jesus my Lord: for whom I have suffered the loss of all things, and do count them but dung, that I may win Christ, and be found in Him, not having mine own righteousness, which is of the law, but that which is through the faith of Christ, the righteousness which is of God by faith: that I may know Him, and the

128

power of His resurrection, and the fellowship of His suffer-ings, being made conformable unto His death; if by any means I might attain unto the resurrection of the dead. Not as though I had already attained... (Philippians 3:7-12).

Paul didn't claim that he had "arrived," even though he wrote two-thirds of the New Testament! "Faith toward God" is knowing that you grow from glory to glory and from faith to faith with God's help. **True faith eliminates stagnant stages from our lives.** It actually eliminates "backsliding" because it constantly encourages us to go on for more of God and His abundance in our lives. The minute you hit the state where you believe you have arrived, something will die inside you! God is always helping us to progress and move on because He is always teaching His people new things. Every generation must hear a fresh word from God so it can grow to greater levels of glory. God is requiring us to grow in Him.

If we catch ourselves saying something like, "I thank God for using me two years ago to love and help so-and-so," then we're living on a harvest from the past. We must continually plant more seed every day. God didn't call us to be "fisherman for a day," or "a farmer for a weekend." Our marriage covenant with God is a lifelong hitch, a permanent commitment to grow in His likeness. He gave us eternal life so we won't have to "retire" our hunger for His presence. One of the ways to greatness is to burn your past laurels and move on. Our prayer must be, "Dear Lord, I thank You for using me then, but what do You want me to do here and now? As long as I have breath to praise You and serve You, I want to use the strength of my days to glorify You!"

"Whatever is on the top of Your priority list, Lord, let it be on mine. Whatever is burning on Your heart, God, I want it to burn on my heart also. Let my life not be squandered on careless, frivolous, and apathetic living when Your divine purpose awaits me. Take the gifts and talents I have been made steward over and use them to bring honor to Your name!"

Faith also has the ability to be content with who it is without being recognized for everything it has done! While rejoicing in God's bounty and the victories of one day, it reaches forward with every bit of its strength for more of God's fullness and glory! It rejoices in truth, it is victorious in trials, it suffers long, and it doesn't give up easily. The God-kind of faith is hungry. True faith keeps on growing and pressing "toward the mark for the prize of the high calling of God in Christ Jesus" (Phil. 3:14)! The best prize we can receive is the high calling of God! That is something to press toward. God supplies His rest so we can continue to soar in the realm of the miraculous with the wings of eagles. God's faith is a consuming fire that is never totally satisfied. It is very progressive.

God wants every local body of believers to rise up in burning zeal and unquenchable faith to become a brilliant lighthouse to their communities, touching countless hurting and lost people with the unforgettable passion and compassion of God!

Faith Believes the Word

Faith makes us one with God and His Word. True biblical faith is never separate from God. Many believers find it hard to understand how they can literally become "one with God." Our "union with God" is hard to fathom at six in the morning when we are facing a harsh reality in the mirror! The truth is that it is simultaneously absolutely impossible and absolutely true! Only God could pull off such a miracle, and He did it at Calvary! Look yourself in the eyes (as soon as you can pry them open) and tell yourself, "God has something good prepared for me today! I'm going to walk in His plan of good works for my life, works that He has prepared for me before the foundation of the world. I will believe that every one of His promises are true for my life. I put my faith in His love for me above the feelings and circumstances that surround me. I release my faith for God's best, for this is the day the Lord has made!"

Subject your body's aches and sleepy emotions to the unchanging Word of God. See yourself in *union* with your Creator. It may take a miracle, but remember that you have one! His name is Jesus, and His miracle at the tomb transforms you in your room. Sleepy or not, you are a miracle walking the earth! According to the authoritative Word of God, you are actually a *conqueror* in Christ. Now be what God says you are!

Lay aside every objection and consider the most important statements about life: God says you are more than a conqueror (see Rom. 8:37). The Bible says *you* are the righteousness of God in Christ Jesus (see 2 Cor. 5:21). These truths become reality to you when you believe what God says about you. This is what God means by having "faith toward God." There is no pride involved— only total dependence on your miracle-working God!

"I don't feel like it, and God knows I certainly don't act like it sometimes, but the Bible says I am a child of God and heir of all the promises. God said it, so I believe it." Your spirit will be encouraged as you consider God's words about you. They will change you. Take no credit for your victories. Always speak the truth. "The truth is, God won the victory for me. God made me His righteousness. God made me His loved one and set His love upon me. That is why I know He will deliver me!" (See Psalm 91:14.)

For we are His workmanship, created in Christ Jesus unto good works, which God hath before ordained that we should walk in them. Wherefore remember, that ye being in time past Gentiles in the flesh, who are called Uncircumcision by that which is called the Circumcision in the flesh made by hands; that at that time ye were without Christ, being

*aliens from the commonwealth of Israel, and strangers from
the covenants of promise, having no hope, and without God
in the world: but now in Christ Jesus ye who sometimes were
far off are made nigh by the blood of Christ. For He is our
peace, who hath made both one, and hath broken down the
middle wall of partition between us; having abolished in His
flesh the enmity, even the law of commandments contained
in ordinances; for to make in Himself of twain one new man,
so making peace; and that He might reconcile both unto
God in one body by the cross, having slain the enmity
thereby: and came and preached peace to you which were
afar off, and to them that were nigh. For through Him we
both have access by one Spirit unto the Father* (Ephesians
2:10-18).

God desires to work through us as His hands, His feet, His eyes,
and His mouth. He has chosen that we be His representatives on
the earth, His workmen and His workmanship. Not only are we the
work of His hands, but we are also called to carry out the very work
He hands us.

We are one spirit with the Lord! That is an awesome thought.
That is a world-changing, life-rearranging thought! God lives in
our inner man. It takes meekness to receive this fact because our
emotions and intellect can't handle it. Every time we sin or make
a mistake, our mind and emotions make us feel separated from God.
By drawing near to God through repentance, forgiveness, and
ultimately restoration, we stay connected and our faith stays strong!

The Book of James provides the key we need to receive what God
says about us and our relationship with Him: "...receive with meekness the engrafted word, which is able to save your souls" (Jas. 1:21).

Our soul (meaning our mind, will, and emotions) must humble
itself before it can do any changing. Our soul is the very "I will" of

132

our personhood. When we try to tell it that it needs changing, sometimes it seems all hell breaks loose. It literally does, for the mind is the battleground of faith. Through humility and in God's love for us, His Word will come and separate our soul from our spirit so we can clearly see where to submit to God's gentle discipline (see Heb. 4:12).

It requires a continual attitude of humility to walk with God in faith. It means subordinating our carnal thoughts and emotions to the principles of God's Word. Performance-based religious rituals and observances easily separate us from God's revealed Word by drawing us toward the "letter of the law" instead of the "Spirit of the law." Holding onto religious traditions or stubborn opinions separate us from His truth. The solution is simple and direct: When we humble ourselves, God will guide us in judgment and wisdom. According to Micah 6:8, the Lord requires us to "do justly, and to love mercy, and to walk humbly with our God." It requires humility to hear His voice and continue to grow in His Word.

Faith Gives Glory to God

When you walk in faith toward God, your life and your lips will continually give the credit and thanksgiving to God. We are "walking in faith toward God" when we give honor where honor is due. True self-esteem comes from knowing that *God has forgiven you and lives in you.* You share your destiny with Jesus Christ Himself! God has invested His life in you. He planted His supernatural gifts within you, and that is where your confidence and pride come from. It is not we who live, but Christ who lives in us (see Gal. 2:20). Abraham gave glory to God because he was fully persuaded that what God had promised, He was able to perform (see Rom. 4:21).

Faith Speaks and Acts

Faith has a voice, and faith has actions to back up what it believes. Ezekiel the prophet described a miraculous vision that still speaks to our lives today:

The hand of the Lord was upon me, and carried me out in the spirit of the Lord, and set me down in the midst of the valley which was full of bones ... Again He said unto me, Prophesy upon these bones, and say unto them, O ye dry bones, hear the word of the Lord. Thus saith the Lord God unto these bones; Behold, I will cause breath to enter into you, and ye shall live: and I will lay sinews upon you, and will bring up flesh upon you, and cover you with skin, and put breath in you, and ye shall live; and ye shall know that I am the Lord. ...and as I prophesied, there was a noise, and behold a shaking, and the bones came together, bone to his bone. And when I beheld, lo, the sinews and the flesh came up upon them, and the skin covered them above: but there was no breath in them. Then said He unto me, Prophesy unto the wind.... So I prophesied as He commanded me, and the breath came into them, and they lived, and stood up upon their feet, an exceeding great army (Ezekiel 37:1,4-10).

Who wants to prophesy to a bunch of bones? That is no way to build a national television ministry, but the ancient prophets of God had to do things like that all the time! God's servants may look foolish, since faith is not understood by the natural mind. The Bible says, "...[Abraham] believed, even God, who quickeneth the dead, and *calleth those things which be not as though they were. Who against hope believed in hope, that he might become the father of many nations...*" (Rom. 4:17-18). Abraham had a voice and he was strong in faith. We need to be like Abraham—and not stagger at the promise of God for our lives! Call things that be not as though they were. Be a fool for Christ and dare to believe what God says about you and His Kingdom. God's destiny for us is greatness. In the Book of Jeremiah, God says, "Call unto Me, and I will answer thee, and shew thee great and mighty things..." (Jer. 33:3). He also said earlier, "For I know the thoughts that I think toward you, saith the Lord, thoughts of peace, and not of evil, to give you an excepted end" (Jer. 29:11). God loves happy endings, and He has planned one just for you! Cast out your doubts, get relief from unbelief, and say yes to becoming everything God has said you are. He is faithful who called you, and will also bring it to pass (see 1 Thess. 5:24).

Chapter 10

Joseph's Secrets

Every experience God gives us, every person he puts in our lives, is the perfect preparation for the future that only he can see. —Corrie ten Boom

When we as the Body of Christ go through a dry season, we need patience, longsuffering, and faith toward God. We may be waiting upon the Lord, but we're still moving ahead. It is in those seasons that God shares *Joseph's secrets* of power with us.

Joseph was a man of vision. If you don't have a vision from God, then do whatever it takes to receive that vision for your personal life! I never met a depressed person who was doing what he or she was called to do. Adversity may arise at any time, but the depression comes when we have no vision, or when we wander outside the vision or calling of God. The Bible declares, "Weeping may endure for a night, but joy cometh in the morning" (Ps. 30:5b).

Blessed is the man whose strength is in Thee; in whose heart are the ways of them. Who passing through the valley of

137

Baca [weeping] *make it a well; the rain also filleth the pools. They go from strength to strength, every one of them in Zion appeareth before God* (Psalm 84:5-7).

God has an endless supply of living water for us that is waiting to flow out of us, even during a dry season. When Jesus met the Samaritan woman at the well, He said something that is crucial to us right now:

Jesus answered and said unto her, If thou knewest the gift of God, and who it is that saith to thee, Give Me to drink; thou wouldest have asked of Him, and He would have given thee living water. … But whosoever drinketh of the water that I shall give him shall never thirst; but the water that I shall give him shall be in him a well of water springing up into everlasting life (John 4:10,14).

Water is the most scarce and valuable substance in any desert country, especially in times of drought. The world outside our church walls is a dry desert, a land of death, disillusionment, desperation, and degeneracy. There are millions of "women of Samaria" longing for a well of hope and life. It is more important than ever for the Church to be a well of living water, springing up into everlasting life, a shining oasis of hope for the world. But what do we do when the drought hits close to home?

Joseph suffered from spiritual droughts most of his life. He learned a few secrets of survival along the way that you and I need to learn. One obvious lesson we can learn from him is that God's purposes are often impossible to "figure out." Joseph would never have walked in the plan of God if he had tried to figure everything out. When you face a trial or a wilderness journey, don't analyze it. Don't nurse it or rehearse it; just curse it! Resist whatever is evil in the situation and submit to God. Allow nothing to deter you from the plan of God for your life. **In every situation, the will of God**

is for you to seek Him with all your heart, and to trust Him in all things.

Seasoned With Time

The secret of productivity in our lives is to *find a cause greater than ourselves* and to give ourselves to it. We need to enter what is called "the dark night of the soul" and begin to wait on the Lord in persistent prayer. When Jewish potters make new pots, they set aside the very best pots and pottery for special treatment. After they put their name on the underside of these extra good pieces, they put them away in a cold, damp room for storage, away from the public view.

It is only when the more selective buyers ask for the "very best" of the potter's products that the craftsman will retrieve the chosen pots from their hidden storage place. He purposely keeps his best work in reserve just for that appointed time when he can happily place it before the buyer and say, "This is the best I have—but it will cost more than the rest." The discriminating buyer will immediately pay the price the potter demands, since these works of art are better than the norm.

The Master Potter may have placed you in a cold storage room for a season while you mature and grow strong in the silent darkness. You can only wait for the appointed time of the Lord when He, with pleasure, places you into His service. To believers, though, the life of faith doesn't always make sense. You may feel lost in that dark night of the soul, seemingly gathering dust in the Lord's storage room of the wilderness. Set your heart and desire on the Master Himself, not merely on the outward activities and blessings of His household. Paul said, "That I may know Him, and the power of His resurrection, and the fellowship of His sufferings, being made conformable unto His death" (Phil. 3:10). I want to know the Lord that way too.

A season of waiting on God makes most of us think, "I've really blown it. I've made so many mistakes that I must be out of the will of God." The Lord says, "No, no. You are not out of My will! You are right in the center of it. It is only by waiting upon Me, however, that I can share with you My sufferings and the blessings they produce." God works according to principle. So often these waiting periods occur because of His emphasis on order and personal priorities. Jesus was mostly likely able to come to the earth to live and die and fulfill His ministry immediately after the fall in Eden. The question is, was it God's timing? Would man have been prepared for His arrival?

Don't allow condemnation to weigh you down in that strange room of captivity. You are being seasoned and matured in God's storeroom of greatness! You are in good company. It happened to Moses. It happened to Elijah and David. It happened to John the Baptist and to Paul. In fact, it even happened to Jesus! All of them spent time in the desert of trials and adversity, and all of them emerged with the vision of God! He is seasoning you right now. You are like a pot of miracle stew doing a slow simmer on the back burner! If you are removed from the heat one minute too early, you won't "come out just right."

Unless a seed falls into the ground and dies, it remains alone; but if it dies it bears much fruit (see Jn. 12:24). The season called the dark night of the soul has a wonderful promise that goes with it. Death always brings forth life. When a seed is hidden in the ground and dies, it will bring forth great fruit.

Here is the answer for loneliness and unfruitfulness. Alone in a prison cell, Jeremiah was prompted by God to "call unto Me, and I will answer thee, and shew thee great and mighty things, which thou knowest not" (Jer. 33:3). When we die to our own personal agendas and go into a season of captivity, we learn what is really important in life. We learn to lean upon God who alone is the answer to our loneliness and unfruitfulness. You'll always remain lonely until you die to the fleshly activities that may satisfy only for a season. You live when you set your mind, thoughts, and emotions on the things that are above (see Col. 3:2).

Captivity can kill you unless you recognize that it is a necessary process of growth. A seed must be hidden and captive to produce life.

In Jeremiah 48:11-12 the Lord speaks of a group of people called Moab. The Word says, "Moab [had] been at ease from his youth, and he hath settled on his lees, and hath not been emptied from vessel to vessel, neither hath he gone into captivity: therefore his taste remained in him, and his scent is not changed. Therefore, behold, the days come, saith the Lord, that I will send him wanderers, that shall cause him to wander, and shall empty his vessels, and break their bottles."

Moab means "rebel." These were a people who were exceedingly proud and arrogant (see Jer. 48:29). God has a process that rids us of that loftiness. Wine passes through a seasoning process, it is emptied from vessel to vessel and goes into (storage) or captivity for a season in order to produce a rich taste and scent. Every individual that God has chosen to become great in His Kingdom must pass through this same seasoning process. If this process is embraced, then the consequences of pride will be avoided. A wandering spirit that invades your personal life, ministry, or church is a result of pride. Pride produces such wandering spirits as unfaithfulness and spiritual adultery. Pride produces a great falling away. God came to help us to die to our fleshly appetites that are contrary to the Word of God and to live to the fruit of the Spirit—love, joy, peace, patience, kindness, goodness, faithfulness, greatness, and self-control. God came to help us to live in an intimate relationship with Him, which produces joy, peace, and righteousness.

Embrace the process of growth and recognize that seasons of captivity are designed to pull you into the promises of God's Word. The Word of God always brings hope. If you ever hear a word without hope, just know it is not from God. Even in captivity God says He knows the plans He has for you: plans of good and not of evil, to give you an expected end (a hope in your later end) (see Jer. 29:11). Find that good word no matter how depraved you feel, and you won't stay a lonely, captive exile.

Is God deepening your spirit like He did Job's? Adversity helps us understand what we are "made of." **God can only trust vessels in key positions of leadership and ministry when they have been proven.** Proven vessels have been oven-baked and refired again and again in the kiln of commitment until they've proven their ability to withstand the pressures and temperature of the fire. Once you cry out, "God, I want to be like You," then you will probably be broken up, made over into a brand-new vessel, and whisked out of the bright light into a deserted and dark back storage room *until the appointed time.* Remember, diamonds were just pieces of coal formed in a dark, pressurized environment.

What is your humility level? How do you react when you are denied justice, put off for a while, or are offended by wrongdoing? Don't jump off the shelf; you are still a handcrafted pot waiting on God. God says, "Just wait there." Moses had to do it. Moses spent 40 years in the wilderness waiting on God after he killed a man in his anger and youthful zeal. He seemed to have all the qualifications to lead his people to freedom. He was raised and trained to rule as a son in Pharaoh's household. He had power, position, and secular preparation, but he lacked the seasoning and character of God. He spent 40 years waiting for his calling to come forth.

Paul was a New Testament copy of Moses. He was a Jew of the Jews, a respected member of the Sanhedrin and a favored student of Gamaliel, the most famous "law professor" in all of Judaism. Paul was on the fast track to success, but he lacked one thing. He lacked the vision of God for his life. After the Lord confronted him on the road to Damascus, this great scholar and Pharisee was shipped off to the wilderness for three years to await the call of God.

It was in isolation and separation that Paul received the direct revelation of Jesus Christ that would transform the New Testament Church! That is why he was a chosen vessel of God. **The vessels destined to bear great and precious anointings are always moved to the back burner of life for a while.** According to the Bible, Paul was called from a life in the temple to a life of tribulation "to be a light of the Gentiles, that thou shouldest be for salvation unto the ends of the earth" (Acts 13:47). Paul was revealed to the Church as a *chosen vessel* only after he had become a *proven vessel.*

Joseph was in training for reigning from his birth, to the pit of slavery, to his fateful encounter with Potiphar's wife, and finally to the day he shared power with mighty Pharaoh. What can we learn from Joseph's life that will help us *today, tonight*, and *tomorrow* in the Potter's back room? Joseph learned three key lessons that helped him move faithfully from the pit to the throne room by God's provision.

Use Humility and Wisdom When Sharing

When the day came that Joseph received a supernatural vision from God, Joseph couldn't wait to share it with others. This man got a lot of criticism for sharing his vision, but the vision was not the problem. Rather, it was his lack of humility and wisdom. Pride goes before a fall. As excited as you may be about your vision, you appear foolishly lofty when sharing it before others with the same ambitions. Rather, do what Mary did. Ponder dreams in your heart until you find those who can run with you in the dream. Even then, be wise and meek in sharing your vision. Others may not be as pure in heart as you assume them to be.

Joseph unwisely shared his vision of rulership with his older brothers and other relatives and friends—and they did not like it. Very few people even claimed to hear from God in those days, and even though Joseph was clearly anointed, his life lacked one of the most important fruits of "seasoning" in the life of faith: humility. Joseph was chosen by God, but he had a painful appointment for a long and dark "night of the soul" to learn firsthand what real humility was.

God requires three things of every person whom He has chosen for service and leadership in His Kingdom: justice, mercy, and humble trust.

The supernatural "calling of God" doesn't negate our will or give us instant maturity. When God calls you into His army, you must go through "boot camp." There are no alternatives to God's basic training in the dry wilderness of adversity. Only tried and proven vessels can be entrusted with the well-being of God's beloved sheep. We may be God's chosen people and a royal and peculiar priesthood, but that doesn't make us any better than anybody else. We're just forgiven human beings filled with the power and anointing of God.

Joseph's lack of *wisdom* led to another nearly fatal mistake: He shared his vision too quickly. God can turn our mistakes into miracles, but it is easier and less painful to learn how to keep our mouths shut until God says to open them! Humility does not even speak on its own account. The Holy Spirit never speaks on His own account. He always prefers to give glory to the Father and the Son. The Holy Spirit is the perfect example of temperance and humility.

When Joseph rashly shared his heavenly vision of his leadership position over his family, his older brothers became insanely jealous. The anointing of God always brings jealousy, but the anointing combined with human mistakes makes things go really bad! That is why it is so important that the first lesson we learn is to be *meek* before God.

Even when we lead God's flock, we should also be followers who are quick to serve one another in humility and meekness of mind. Pride is destroyed when we esteem others better than ourselves. When you want to see someone else's ministry or blessings exceed your own, you are bearing the good fruit of humility and love.

Joseph had the *anointing* of God, but he added *meekness* to his character after he made the mistake of sharing his vision too soon, was thrown into a pit, and sold into slavery by his own brothers.

Great People Seek Out Mentors

The second thing Joseph learned is that great people are always looking for mentors for wise counsel. Joseph had a secret from God's own heart; he knew he was called, but his impetuousness led to a fall. Joseph didn't have access to Spirit-filled men of God for counsel, but we do. One of the most important lessons we can learn as we grow up in God is that we shouldn't share everything we know with everybody. The Bible says, "A fool uttereth all his mind: but a wise man keepeth it in till afterwards" (Prov. 29:11). God puts practical people in our lives, such as pastors and elders, to provide sound advice and confidential counsel.

If you are a visionary with a dream from God, submit your dream to godly counselors, like your pastor or spiritual leadership, before you enthusiastically share it with everyone near you. The Book of Proverbs says, "...in the multitude of counsellors there is safety" (Prov. 11:14).

My husband Tom is one of the spiritual overseers God has put in my life, and I honor him as my husband, my counselor, and my pastor. He has a vision for ministry, and so we minister together sometimes. While he is very gifted, he is also steady, practical, and very meek. He is a quiet man, for he has learned that he doesn't need to share all his secrets. He keeps them inside and God gives him His favor. For the chosen vessels, God is the one who brings forth *promotion* in their lives.

Poor Joseph made some mistakes, but they are ones we can learn from. When Joseph was betrayed by his brothers, he learned the hard way that the devil comes to destroy the foundations of trust. We must protect our fellowship with the brethren.

What are the three most important things you long for in relationships? Most of us long for joy, trust, and understanding love. We all want friends and trusted confidants who will say, "Hey, I understand what you're saying. I hear you." We're not just looking for someone who can understand us. We also want someone who can be trusted with our secrets! There is no way we can appreciate a "friend" who trots down the street to tell all or even some of our secrets to others after we have shared with them our suffering and pain in confidence.

Joseph Learned How to Forgive

The third and most important lesson Joseph learned was the need for forgiveness. This may be the most strategic truth we can learn in the grand plans of God. Hardly any other area better reflects the beauty of God's own nature than His ability to forgive us and restore us to His fellowship! This is the heart of the process whereby He "conforms us" to the image of His Son (see Rom. 8:29). If we don't forgive, God can't forgive us!

How do you deal with betrayal in your marriage, your friendships, in the local church, or in the workplace? God commands us to deal with it in the same way He does: with *forgiveness*. **The only way to restore broken trust and a defiled relationship is**

through forgiveness. Fortunately we can call upon God to help us, and He quickly responds. As I said before, it is far better for us to be merciful than for us to be proven right.

Joseph landed in one impossible situation after another following his brothers' betrayal. First he was thrown in a desert pit and sold into slavery. Then he was "sold" to Potiphar and wrongly imprisoned for "doing the right thing" when he resisted the adulterous advances of Potiphar's wife! After he helped out a fellow prisoner, his good deed was "forgotten" and seemingly ignored for years while Joseph rotted in a dark dungeon far from the light of day. Yet this man kept rising to the occasion because his days in the "pit crew" had taught him valuable lessons about humility and wisdom. He was morally impeccable. He had learned his lessons well and had become a man with a perfect heart before God. He was now in line for a promotion!

He may have thought he was "ready for the ministry" the day he recieved his heavenly vision, but not according to God. Joseph still had some lessons to learn about human nature. The schooling began in a sandy pit, but the intensity really picked up in Potiphar's bedroom! He quickly learned that if the devil can't get you to sin morally, he'll try to falsely accuse you! Joseph also learned that the Lord was his defender. Like Joseph, I've faced the fear of man and I've dealt with it. I have felt the serious pain of rejection. But I always try to remember that when I stand before God someday, He will ask me to give account of my words and deeds. Man will not be my judge then; God will be my judge. I want to receive a crown of life on that glorious day.

When you suffer the pain of lies and false accusations and you feel the sting of rejection, rejoice in God's unconditional love for you. Rise up in the Spirit of God and say, "My God has made me able." Allow the Holy Spirit to minister to you, to pierce through that darkness of rejection and bring you the healing balm of Gilead.

He will remind you that you have dignity in Him. You have a holy purpose and a divine destiny that no one can take from you!

In the end, God did promote Joseph. The lessons he learned later blessed both the nation of Egypt and the children of Israel, when Joseph wisely *prepared for the drought* ahead of time and saved the lives of millions through his wise stewardship. His dream of leadership was fulfilled, but in his maturity, it was marked by forgiveness, mercy, and restoration rather than by domination. Remember the lessons of Joseph every time you find yourself in a dry season. If you have prepared well in God's bounty, you will not only preserve yourself, but also bless the lives of everyone who comes to you for refreshment in times of spiritual famine. It is your destiny!

Part IV

The Evidence of Greatness

Chapter 11

Marked by God

Dost thou wish to rise? Begin by descending. You plan a tower that shall pierce the clouds? Lay first the foundation of humility. —St. Augustine

Years ago, a young couple were informed that they were going to have a baby. Like most parents, they were elated. While the little one developed over the next eight months, they dreamed together. Was the baby a boy or a girl? A Little League baseball player or a ballerina? Perhaps a future president?

When the baby was born, they were shocked to see on her face a very long, deformed red mark. Although she could very easily have grown up psychologically damaged, she did not. Her smart parents told her from day one that the mark on her face was the spot where the angels had kissed her. She always remembered she was marked by God.

The true evidence of Kingdom greatness in your life is being marked by God. When God puts His sign upon you for extraordinary accomplishments and supernatural achievements, satan also targets you, but he does so for destruction. Being marked by God means you have been chosen to enter a realm of God's anointing that most people don't even know exists. The Bible describes these chosen people as "certain" Christians because they are totally surrendered to the purpose, principles, plans, and pursuits of God's Kingdom. They are marked by God as His chosen vessels and marked by the devil's "hit men" as "certain" Christians who need to be destroyed.

When we see Jesus, we see the perfect example of greatness. He evidenced the authority that comes with greatness by driving demon spirits out of people's lives. He was given such authority because of His submissive, humble obedience to His Father. His act of humbling Himself as God to become human, as well as living in perfect obedience to God's Word, gave Him the authority to rule over and command the ruler of this world and his demons. That example has been set before us as today's sons and daughters of God in order to bring the ministry of Jesus to the world. We must know that living in the light of God's Word stills the avenger, satan. We see this same authority over demon spirits operating through the life of Paul and other great leaders throughout Church history. Demons knew Jesus. Demons knew Paul. Are you known in hell?

Then certain of the vagabond Jews, exorcists, took upon them to call over them which had evil spirits the name of the Lord Jesus, saying, We adjure you by Jesus whom Paul preacheth. And there were seven sons of one Sceva, a Jew, and chief of the priests, which did so. And the evil spirit answered and said, Jesus I know, and Paul I know; but who are ye? (Acts 19:13-15)

God marks certain Christians for greatness. He loves everyone, even unbelievers who reject Him. He has even forgiven them through Jesus' sacrifice, but only "certain" Christians are marked by Him. Those who are marked by God are known in the very corridors of hell. They evidence a deadness to the will of the flesh and a living commitment to God's will unmatched in the earth. They are so full of God that to touch them is to touch God! They are chosen.

These "certain" Christians have sold out to God to the degree that their own lives are literally nonexistent. They are bondservants to the Lord Jesus Christ. The highest level of Christianity you can rise to in this life is to make yourself a bondservant of the Lord Jesus. Paul consistently called himself a bondservant of the Lord, although he knew he was one in the Spirit with Him—a son of God. Bondservants instantly do whatever God asks without wondering or asking why. They are the epitome of trust and obedience because of their humility and desire to please their master. These Christians are like the Special Force commandos or the Secret Service agents who have vowed to risk their lives in order to protect and preserve the security of their country.

There is constant warfare in the heavenlies over these certain chosen people of God. They are the devil's worst nightmare. Just when satan thought Jesus was gone for good, here comes a whole army of Godlike earth-men filled with Spirit power, divine authority, and the nature of God. It would have given him a heart attack, had he a heart! In fact, he has no mind, or he wouldn't persist in a battle that he has no hope of winning. His plans are doomed for failure. His day of judgment is almost at hand! Until that day arrives, however, he continues to assault the godly forces that demonstrate God's Kingdom and evidence the greatness of their Master, Jesus Christ.

...And He called to the man clothed with linen, which had the writer's inkhorn by his side; and the Lord said unto him, Go through the midst of the city, through the midst of Jerusalem, and set a mark upon the foreheads of the men

*that sigh and that cry for all the abominations that be done
in the midst thereof* (Ezekiel 9:3-4).

There are certain Christians marked by God because they pray,
cry, intercede, and travail over the abominations that are done in
the nations and the cities of the world. They have been set apart to
"stand in the gap" for God's people and to lead them to become
great in God's Kingdom. God looks at these prayer warriors and
says, "Don't touch My anointed; do them no harm! They are Mine
and they bear My mark! If you touch them, you are touching Me!"
(See Psalm 105:15.) This militia of ministers stands on the front
lines of spiritual battle and assaults the forces of darkness. They
drive back the spiritual wickedness and cry out to God to forgive
the sins of their nations and cities.

**In this dimension of greatness comes a selfless prayer life of
intercession for the lives of other people.** They have forgotten
about their own needs. They have become dead to the problems that
would have caused most well-meaning Christians to bail out. They
have put their trust in God for the deliverance and restoration they
need and go to battle on behalf of their brothers and sisters. These
"marked ones" suffer much, but they seem impervious to the fiery
darts of the enemy because they are already dead to the things he
can throw at them. They no longer fear death or persecution. They
boldly declare, "Whom shall I fear?"

If you have this evidence of God's mark upon your life, then
God has a special covering upon your life. Your times are in His
hands. No evil can befall you and no plague or destruction can come
near your life. You may suffer some attacks or even disasters, but
you will not be stopped in your mission until you have completed
your purpose and fulfilled God's plan on the earth. Being marked
by God means you are divorced from the attachments of this world.
Your dependence on God keeps you seeking His divine provision

to sustain your every need and supply. The devil can take nothing from you, or he would have to steal from God.

Another evidence of these certain Christians is their ability to lay aside personal accomplishments and boast only in what God has accomplished. They have nothing to brag about regarding their own personal achievements. It is God's ability that becomes the focus of activities and of doing and overcoming even the greatest human weakness and failure. In doing so, God takes those defeated areas and resurrects them into supernatural Kingdom victories! For the "certain" Christians, the battle is won before the battle has ever begun.

When God chooses those whom He will mark in His Kingdom, He looks for a characteristic called yieldedness. He picks those whom He can put on the potter's wheel and make into a great vessel. Once they are chosen for God's shaping process, they are placed upon the wheel to be shaped into a special design and purpose. On the potter's wheel is where the marks of greatness can be seen forming in a vessel. Some vessels don't stay on the wheel long enough to even be marked as a chosen vessel. Many are called (placed on the wheel), but few are chosen (conformed into His image). If the vessel decides to get off the potter's wheel before completion, it is no good to the potter. He takes it and throws it in a place called the potter's field.

The potter's field is where Judas ended up—in a forgotten grave, buried under millions of pieces of broken pottery. That's what happens when you don't yield to God and choose to follow your own way. On the other hand, you can't be broken or broken-hearted if you learn to bend or yield to the Lord.

Christians who yield to God bear His mark. Peter yielded to God. He made some mistakes and blew it in front of everyone, but he was yielded to God. He was a "certain" Christian who helped turn the world upside down. Peter rolled up his sleeves and went to work for the Lord. Even in the face of failure, he knew God had forgiven him. He got right back out there knowing it wasn't him, but Christ who lived within him.

Faith is a mark of a chosen vessel. It takes faith to go beyond our own fears and selfish desires to become a vessel useful for the Master. Faith doesn't limit God to what He can or can't do in our lives. It gives Him freedom to be who He is and to do what He wants to do through us. This humble attitude of trust gives the Master Potter creative license to form and fashion us into any shape He so desires. He has those chosen vessels "marked" for a special purpose and occasion known only by Him.

Boldness is another mark of a chosen vessel. Those marked by God aggressively pursue God's call upon their lives. Their strength of spirit causes them to break through obstacles to their mission and overcome the problems that invade their efforts toward Kingdom work. They give themselves to a selfless life of giving through prayer and service. Financial problems just become opportunities to give their way into the blessings of God's abundance. Marked believers fear neither man nor beast, not even death. They boldly proclaim God's Word, saying, "O death, where is thy sting? O grave, where is thy victory?" (1 Cor. 15:55) Their passion is to save the lost, heal the sick, restore the fallen, and comfort the hurting.

Marked Christians are single-minded. They have an unquenchable passionate pursuit for the things of God. They spend time in God's presence more than anywhere else. Negative thinking and speaking is far from their lives. There is no room in their hearts or minds for things that displease their Master. They move in unity with God's flow of construction to His house.

These certain marked Christians wreak havoc on the enemy's camp. The mark of the Master on their lives is like a holy disease or a consuming fire that is contagious and infectious, and is fueled and spread by the unapproachable light of Almighty God. In satan's dark domain, these marked Christians are dangerous and their work devastating.

There are other Christians so oblivious and carnal that instead of being marked by God, they unknowingly become the devil's "hit man." They are so consumed with jealousy of the "marked ones" that they don't realize they become agents for the devil's dirty work. The devil knows that if he can get someone to betray or do his work in disguise behind the lines, he will be most effective. Rather than being marked by God, these "uncertain" Christians are marked by satan. These are the spots, the tares, the wolves, and those causing the bitter defilement that contaminates so many churches and Christian relationships.

Do marked believers ever feel dry or deserted? Of course! They are often assigned desert duty in a dry place. They fight through, being faithful, and defend their post through their dedication to God's purpose. Every marked person carries battle scars on his or her body. Follow someone who walks with a limp because he or she has been through the battle and has come out fighting. Such people can describe what it is like to feel stranded in a dry and empty place. They are never content to just let things happen, though. When things get so bad that it looks like there's no hope, they get fired up even more. They love the part of the story where they get to describe the smell and feel of a soon-coming rain! They love to tell about the moment they plunged themselves into the rich, cool water of the Father's presence to emerge fully refreshed and anointed once again.

Those marked by God rule and reign with Him. They are given resources and visions. They are prophets pioneering in unreached areas for Kingdom advancement. They are the ones leading the charge against the devil's division and deception of our churches and families. They are constantly being repairers of the breach and restorers of the paths to dwell in. They overcome evil with good.

The vessels that God has His eye on are the yielded vessels kneeling in submissive obedience to God's every word and whim. These are the ones who bear God's mark of humility, justice, mercy, and greatness. This is His army of intercessors willing to weep before God's altar on behalf of those under the devil's deception. They attack the very gates of hell in a holy passion of fire from on high! God says, "I have marked your heart for greatness. You are a chosen vessel on which I have engraved My name. Now is the appointed time for your life to fulfill its true purpose and meaning for existence. You have come into the Kingdom for such a time as this. Take your place in the assembly of the marked ones and begin the work of greatness prepared for you before the foundation of the world."

Chapter 12

The Grateful Dead

Becoming grateful makes us "great full."

For ye are dead, and your life is hid with Christ in God (Colossians 3:3).

And being found in fashion as a man, he humbled himself, and became obedient unto death, even the death of the cross (Philippians 2:8).

As God's end-time overcomers destined for greatness, we must come to a full realization that our old lives are dead and that we are to walk in the newness of God's life. Paul said, "I live; yet not I, but Christ liveth in me" (Gal. 2:20). Our lives are dead to the things of this world. We no longer need to be diverted from the divine course God has set for us. As the "living dead" who walk in the Spirit, soulish battles of envy, insult, and offense are just a memory of fleshly weakness gone to the grave. We've been embalmed with a supernatural power to overcome all the devil's hellish tactics. Our soulish graveclothes have come off and a living spirit has been resurrected.

The miracle of the New Covenant is that we are now the dwelling place that God inhabits. We are truly God's home. In the Old Covenant, God's dwelling place was a regular tent or temple.

How amiable are Thy tabernacles, O Lord of hosts! ... Blessed are they that dwell in Thy house: they will be still praising Thee. Selah (Psalm 84:1,4).

The word translated as "tabernacles" in the Hebrew means "a residence." It sometimes was used to describe a shepherd's hut, but it also means "a grave." The tabernacle of God is literally a grave. It is more than just a place where dead things are buried. It is a place where dead things find newness of life in Christ Jesus! The Word of God declares, "Old things are passed away; behold, all things are become new" (2 Cor. 5:17b).

Once we are in Christ Jesus, we become dead to this world and God "buries" everything we have been in the past. We are a tabernacle and have been changed from a grave to a living dwelling place of God Almighty! We are the tabernacles David spoke about in Psalm 84:1! When we come to God, He doesn't just give us a second chance; He gives us a brand-new start. We are a new creation, a new dwelling place. God put all our failures under the blood of Jesus. We must keep our mind on His justifying work that changed us from an old dead tomb to a living, breathing, dwelling place of a holy God.

David's greatest desire was to be in the "tabernacle" of God. As God continually draws us to Himself, He builds that tabernacle inside us as His dwelling place. God only uses the best materials for His construction. His materials are washed in the blood, refined in the refiner's fire, and tested in the crucible of affliction. When we bring God the best, we can trust Him for the rest.

Rather than recount our old life of sin, God commands us to remember the good things He has put within us and to be thankful for what He's done. The grateful dead, that's what we are! We are a mighty nation of grateful dead people who have been raised from the grave by the Spirit of God.

Remember all the things God has brought you through and what He's set you free from. Lay aside the entangling memories of your past life and put it under the cleansing blood of Jesus. Then all the oppressive thoughts and emotions of guilt and condemnation will lift and your strength will return. There's always hope in God and in His promises for you. If people can't see any hope in their future, they rapidly lose their thankfulness. One major problem we face in the Church is becoming unthankful. Ingratitude sets in when all we can see are the cares and responsibilities of our day and we forget the fact that God is alive and dwells in our hearts.

When we lose our thankfulness, strange things begin to happen in our lives. Our minds become dark and confused as to what is really true about life and God. Our hearts become hardened and we are no longer sensitive to God's voice or to the needs and hurts of others around us. The apostle Paul warned the believers in Rome, "Because that, when they knew God, they glorified Him not as God, neither were thankful; but became vain in their imaginations, and their foolish heart was darkened" (Rom. 1:21).

The "grateful dead" have attitudes of gratitude. In fact, they have what the Bible calls "dove's eyes." That means they can only see the thing directly in front of them and nothing on either side. They look only to the One they love and honor as their Beloved. A grateful attitude honors God, and God honors a grateful heart. Gratefulness is looking to God with praise and thanksgiving for what He has done. Gratefulness is not mindful of what it doesn't have, but of what it does have! This attitude is not only positive, but it is also very powerful in the scope of greatness.

Grateful Dead Hall of Fame

The Bible has a divine record of what I call the "Grateful Dead Hall of Fame."

John the Baptist was one of the "grateful dead." When he saw Jesus, he told his followers, "He must increase, but I must *decrease*" (Jn. 3:30). Most of us would rather hold on to our ministries, but John the Baptist was basically telling his disciples, "No, don't follow me anymore. Follow Him; He is the light of the world." John's life and ministry always pointed toward Jesus the Messiah. John had the dignity to say by his actions, "I've done what God has asked; I'm grateful for the opportunity to serve God. I'm going to move on to a higher calling." That's what he did.

Abraham is one of the most famous members of this hall of fame. A mighty man of faith with an incredible promise from God, he made a lot of difficult trips to the mountain of trial before his life was over. He nearly sacrificed his only son in obedience to God, but God met him there on the mountain and personally provided a ram in Isaac's place.

Abraham longed for the altar of God. When Abraham was preparing ropes to bind Isaac to the altar on that mountain, Isaac could have run. I believe there was a supernatural faith at work in him too. They both believed and trusted Jehovah Jireh, "the God who provides." Their example demonstrates the deep truth that *the death of a blessing does not mean the death of your worship*. Isaac was Abraham's greatest blessing, yet Abraham was prepared to obey God in worship, even if it meant killing his most prized blessing. Abraham is one of the most honored people among the grateful dead. The hope set before Abraham and Isaac that day was the hope that gave them the strength to worship God in the midst of persecution and heartache, and in the probable death of Abraham's greatest blessing.

David was a man after God's own heart because he made the worship of God his *lifestyle*! He literally "delighted himself in the Lord" and received "the desires of his heart" (see Acts 13:22; Ps. 37:4). That word *delight* means "to be pliable, movable, and bendable" in the hands of God. Worship is a lifestyle. Worship is bowing to the will of God and preferring Him above all things and all people. Worship creates delight, and delight molds our hearts until we, like David, become whatever God wants us to be! If David had to be a shepherd, he was a shepherd. If he had to be a king, he was a king. If he had to be a prophet, he was a prophet. If he had to be a wandering minstrel, he would be a wandering minstrel. Most of the magnificent psalms of David were written during the difficult 15 years he spent on the run from Saul's armies, hiding in the caves and among the rocks!

David was haunted many times with doubts in the wilderness. He must have asked himself, "Am I really anointed by God? Am I really called by God? Why have I been forced to run and hide for years, sleeping on hard rocks and swatting bats in dark and damp caves if I am so anointed and special?" Take heart if you feel like you are stuck on a mountain or buried in a dark cave right now: David's most beautiful and inspiring psalms were born in the darkness of despair.

If we remain pliable in the hands of the Lord, He will protect us from evil men and the traps of the enemy. **If you are pliable in God's hands, He will give you the desires of your heart!**

Ezekiel is a charter member of the "grateful dead" as well, and he was one of the first to see the dead army in action! (See Ezekiel 37 again.) This was the prophet God commanded to prophesy to a pile of dry bones in a desert. Perhaps you are living with some dry bones in your life, your home, or your church. According to the Word of God, your Maker loves you, and He has made great plans for you. You need to hear the word of the Lord—He is speaking life to your dry bones right now! He cries out with the same power and authority that stirred the bones before Ezekiel. He speaks with the same confident tone that forced the decayed body of Lazarus out of the grave. He cries out, "Awake, O sleeper!" The light of

Christ is shining on you. It is a new day, and you are being resurrected to join the army of the grateful dead!

Blessed is the man whose strength is in Thee; in whose heart are the ways of them. Who passing through the valley of Baca [weeping] make it a well; the rain also filleth the pools. They go from strength to strength, every one of them in Zion appeareth before God (Psalm 84:5-7).

When we discussed Joseph's secrets for survival in the desert, we talked about the valley of "Baca," or weeping. Now look closely at the next part of that passage: "Who passing through the valley of Baca [weeping] make it a well; the rain also filleth the pools." God is saying, "You will run out of water while you are in this desert place, but I have a plan for you. I want you to dig a great big hole. In other words, I want you to dig a grave." Naturally, you and I will want to register a polite protest. "But God, You aren't going to leave me here to die, are You? I thought You said You would never leave me or forsake me! Now You're asking me to dig my own grave?" Naturally we get the answer we expected from an unchanging God: "Dig it. As you worship Me from your grave of tears, weakness, failure, and emptiness, the living water of My presence will transform your grave into pools of cool refreshing that will revive all who come near!" My friend, that is God's word to you today! I don't care what situation you face. You can put any name on your desert that you want, but you serve a God who is "more than enough," and it is His delight to turn your desert hole—the grave of the grateful dead—into a shining oasis that continually springs up unto eternal life! Paul said, "When I am weak, then am I strong" (2 Cor. 12:10). Don't be afraid to weep before the Lord. It is the broken and contrite heart that He will not deny. He can turn your tears into pools of refreshing.

The Samaritan woman who met Jesus at "Jacob's well" in the Book of John found a continual well that not only transformed the desert of her life, but also turned her hometown upside down! Once she tasted the living water that Jesus had to offer, she couldn't be satisfied with anything else! Jesus unveiled one of the deepest truths in the New Testament to this woman:

> *But the hour cometh, and now is, when the true worshippers shall worship the Father in spirit and in truth: for the Father seeketh such to worship Him. God is a Spirit: and they that worship Him must worship Him in spirit and in truth* (John 4:23-24).

Jesus changes people. This woman boldly returned to her city with the news of her encounter at the well. She came to an ancient well empty, and left with an eternal well springing up in her heart! Once she met Jesus, she began to change everyone she met! It should be the same way with us. Wherever we go—even during our dry times and desert stays—we can turn empty places and graves into water-filled sanctuaries!

Gratefulness: A Matter of Focus

All of us can find ourselves in a place of desolation if we turn our eyes away from His glory and onto our own story. Even the great prophet Elijah landed in a desolate place when he failed to be grateful. Elijah's tough place was called Mount *Horeb*, which means, of course, "mountain of desolation." Elijah fled to Mount Horeb because he was afraid of a renegade woman who had threatened to kill him. His thoughts were focused on Jezebel, not on his miraculous victory over the 450 prophets of Baal and the 400 prophets of the groves who ate at Jezebel's table. He had no idea how silly he looked in God's eyes. Only a few days earlier, this same great man of faith and power had dared to mock 450 angry, violent, and blood-covered priests of a demonic deity in front of thousands of people. Now he was cowering at the words of one controlling woman who was painting her face in the city of Jezreel.

(See First Kings 18:17-41; 19:1-2.) If he could have heard the words of Jesus, he would have been heartbroken. Like Jerusalem, he was hiding on Mount Horeb, the mountain of desolation. (It is interesting to see that Mount Horeb is called "the mount of God" in First Kings 19:8.) Only days before, Elijah had triumphed over his enemies on Mount Carmel, which means "the mountain of fruitfulness"!

Why did Elijah move so quickly from fruitfulness to desolation on a deserted mountaintop? Had God changed? Absolutely not. Had His enemies changed or increased? No, Jezebel had always hated the prophets of the God of Israel. Now that all her heathen prophets had been killed, she was in the definite minority. Only one thing had changed: Elijah's attitude in seeking the face of God.

Elijah turned his eyes away from Jehovah God to look at himself. In only one day, he became so depressed, lonely, and worried that he prayed in desperation, "It is enough; now, O Lord, take away my life; for I am not better than my fathers" (1 Kings 19:4b). God responded to His prophet's collapse in failure by sending an angel to encourage and strengthen him. Elijah didn't know it, but he had an appointment with God in the wilderness. After 40 days of fasting and praying and his encounter with God, Elijah's subsequent attitude changed and he found new strength, new vision, and a *chosen marked one* in whom he could pass along his anointing!

You may be "chosen by God" and may live the life of the "grateful dead," yet still be depressed and down at times. The Bible has good news for you! "For God is not unrighteous to forget your work and labour of love, which ye have shewed toward His name, in that ye have ministered to the saints, and do minister" (Heb. 6:10). God is always thinking about you. Desolation can only enter our lives when we turn our focus away from the person and the purposes of God. **Wrong attitudes produce wrong fruit.** In the same way, a controlling individual pursuing the work of the Holy Spirit will produce twisted fruit tainted with fear.

Paul was a single man who perhaps was never married. Although he probably had no natural children, he was responsible to pray over an ever-growing family of young believers, a family stretched across the entire Roman Empire. He endured suffering, shipwreck, persecution, and even stoning—but God raised him up. You can't lose with God. The devil found out the hard way that he just couldn't kill Paul because it wasn't God's time yet! He was a man with a mission from God, and nothing was going to stop him. They tried to kill him, but he always came back to haunt them.

Thrice was I beaten with rods, once was I stoned, thrice I suffered shipwreck, a night and a day I have been in the deep; in journeyings often, in perils of waters, in perils of robbers, in perils by mine own countrymen, in perils by the heathen, in perils in the city, in perils in the wilderness, in perils in the sea, in perils among false brethren; in weariness and painfulness, in watchings often, in hunger and thirst, in fastings often, in cold and nakedness. Beside those things that are without, that which cometh upon me daily, the care of all the churches. Who is weak, and I am not weak? who is offended, and I burn not? If I must needs glory, I will glory in the things which concern mine infirmities. The God and Father of our Lord Jesus Christ, which is blessed for evermore, knoweth that I lie not (2 Corinthians 11:25-31).

And He said unto me, My grace is sufficient for thee: for My strength is made perfect in weakness. Most gladly therefore will I rather glory in my infirmities, that the power of Christ may rest upon me (2 Corinthians 12:9).

Let Paul's words encourage you. When you are weak in body or will, you can allow God to be strong in you. Most of the time,

God has been waiting for you to finally get to that point! God is showing us many ways to be grateful. The children of Israel were ungrateful and they spent entire decades wandering in circles through the desolation of the wilderness only a few miles from the Promised Land! Paul, on the other hand, was fruitful in spite of impossible circumstances.

Go to the Highest Level

In our God's universe (which seems backwards from our bent perspective), the highest level of Christian achievement in this world is to be called a *bondservant of the Lord*! Although you are rightfully a son or daughter of God, you lay down your rights and reputation and choose to be the servant of all. That's what it means to be a bondservant! Humble Esther is listed in the Bible's great "Grateful Dead Hall of Fame" because she made no claim to fame. She made no boast of strength, wisdom, virtue, or power. Her only hope was in the God of Israel. She was a reluctant heroine who did the right thing at the right time—even though it could have cost her life.

Esther was so young and naive when God put her in that place of glory as the new queen that she could have been overwhelmed by her newfound wealth, power, position, prestige, and the pampering that goes with it. Praise God, that young woman never forgot who she was. She never ceased to be grateful to her "Uncle" Mordecai for raising her. She never ceased to be grateful to God or to remember her duty to her Jewish race. God didn't "mark" her because she was physically beautiful; He chose her because He saw what was in her heart. He chose Esther because she would face death itself if God asked her to do it—and He did. In the end, humble Esther braved a possible death to deliver her people from certain death.

All the martyrs who died for the cause of Christ were immersed in the Person and purpose of God so strongly that they were willing to lay down their lives. Their focus wasn't on martyrdom; it was on Christ Jesus. They were so busy being grateful for His love that they willingly laid down their lives like sacrificial lambs. On the other hand, we don't like suffering, and most of us don't understand it; but the Bible goes straight to the heart of the matter:

It is a faithful saying: For if we be dead with Him, we shall also live with Him: if we suffer, we shall also reign with Him: if we deny Him, He also will deny us (2 Timothy 2:11-12).

The apostle and martyr Andrew was the brother of Peter. In *Foxe's Christian Heroes and Martyrs* the true story of his obedient sacrificial death is recorded.[1]

Andrew preached the gospel to many Asiatic nations. At Patrae, in Greece, the governor of the country threatened him with death for preaching against the idols which he worshpped; but St. Andrew fearlessly continued to tell the people of Christ. He was therefore sentenced to be crucified on a cross made of two pieces of wood of equal length, the ends of which were fixed in the ground. He was fastened to it, not with nails, but with cords, so that his death might be more slow.

An ancient writer tells of the apostle's sublime courage and fearlessness in the following words: "When Andrew saw the cross prepared, he never changed countenance or color, as the weakness of moral man is wont to do; neither did his blood shrink; neither did he fail in his speech; his body fainted not; neither was his mind molested; his understanding did not fail him; but out of the abundance of his

---

1. *Foxe's Christian Heroes and Martyrs of the World* (Philadelphia, Pennsylvania: Charles Foster Publishing Co., 1907), p. 30.

heart his mouth did speak, and fervent charity did appear in his words. He said, 'O cross, most welcome and oft-looked for; with a willing mind, joyfully and desirously, I come to thee, being the scholar of Him who did hang on thee; because I have been always thy lover, and have longed to embrace thee!' "

St. Andrew hung upon the cross three whole days, suffering dreadful pain, but continuing constantly to tell people around him of the love of Jesus Christ. The people as they listened to him began to believe his words, and asked the governor to let him be taken down from the cross. Not liking to refuse them, he at last ordered the ropes to be cut, but when the last cord was severed, the body of the apostle fell to the ground quite dead.

I don't know how many churches would be filled on Sunday morning if the congregations were being observed by a whole bunch of antagonistic people with guns, but it was in that kind of atmosphere that the early Church was formed! That's the kind of stuff the first century believers were made of. Their commitment to Christ was no light matter. They were willing to live for God and, if necessary, they were willing to die for Him (many of them did). They were so grateful for what God had done in saving them that they were willing to face the fires of persecution and adversity. Are you so grateful to the Lord that you are willing to endure hardship for the sake of the Kingdom of God? **God uses people who are willing to take His mark and stand out from the crowd.**

You may never be called to lay down your life, but you may be asked to sacrificially provide a meal like the little boy who gave Jesus his lunch to feed a crowd of strangers. You may be required to humiliate yourself on the floor by honoring a man or woman of God "in front of your betters" like the woman with the alabaster box filled with ointment. You may even be "accidentally forced" to carry the cross of the Savior up a rugged road of passion and pain. No matter what your point of obedience may be, God knows your name and has prepared you for such a time as this! Rise up in gratefulness and pursue the presence of the Lord with all your might! You are not alone—all those grateful dead who have gone before you are cheering you on in the presence of your King! All it may take is one act of faith or one kind deed to fulfill an eternal destiny that will bring the untold blessings of God upon your life!

Jesus is seeking for union with His people. He desires a bride so passionately that He spends all His time praying for her. What better covering could we have? We need not concentrate on dying to the flesh when we are living with Jesus. Walking with Jesus produces such an intimacy with Him that you just don't have time for anything that doesn't make Him happy. Money, man, and ministry can never replace your intimate relationship with Jesus! If you want to get high—go to the Most High!

That secret place is a place of covering. Jesus says that if we dwell in that place of intimacy we will have God's all-powerful presence protecting us. Then everything that happens to us must pass before God before it can happen to us. Stay tight with Jesus!

Greatness is waiting for those who are grateful, for those who can be thankful enough for what they have been given that all they can do is give it away! When we take the risk of dying to our own life and sow what we have into making someone else great, we become one of the Grateful Dead. Becoming grateful makes us "great full." We have dug our grave and received our life back again! This time it's not a life of earthly weakness and confusion, but a powerful, joyful life of greatness in God's Kingdom. Rise up in His greatness today and be a part of this faceless generation.

Prayers

If you desire to know the greatness of our God and to rise above a normal human existence, where miracles become a way of life, then pray this prayer with me. If you've never asked Jesus to be Lord of your life, pray this prayer from your heart:

Dear Father, my life hasn't been what You would like it to be. I stand guilty and separated from You, having gone my own way. I desire to change today and to live in a super-natural relationship with You. Please take me as I am and forgive my past ignorance and rebellion. I ask Jesus to come into my heart and be Lord over my life. I accept the forgive-ness and His grace to walk a life pleasing to Him. In Jesus' name. Amen.

You may have already received Jesus as your Lord and Savior, yet you know your Christian life has been less than what you know is possible in Christ Jesus. If you sense a need to walk more fully in God's justice, mercy, and humble trust, and you're tired of life as it is, then pray with me:

Dear Father, I know there's a depth to my relationship with You and with others that I have never known. Please, Lord Jesus, fill my life with all that is most important to You. Help me to relate to You and to others with a new measure of Your greatness. Let justice, mercy, and Your humble trust be upon my mind and heart. I believe that You have strength-ened my inner man so I can release Your Spirit-life, making me a part of this faceless generation. In Jesus' name. Amen and Amen. Let it be.

Additional Resources From Lori Wilke

MUSIC CASSETTES/CD'S

CASSETTES

Here I Am	$10.00
Hand In Hand	$10.00
Keep The Flame Burning	$10.00

COMPACT DISCS

Here I Am	$15.00
Hand In Hand	$15.00

TEACHING TAPES

The Baptism Into Fire	(4 tapes)	$20.00
Becoming God's Beloved	(4 tapes)	$20.00
Prayer Warriors Arise!	(4 tapes)	$20.00
The Costly Anointing	(4 tapes)	$20.00
Day of the Living Dead	(4 tapes)	$20.00
Women of Trust	(3 tapes)	$15.00
Rejection and Grief	(3 tapes)	$15.00
Abomination of Condemnation	(3 tapes)	$15.00
You Can Face The Fire	(3 tapes)	$15.00
Obtaining Honor From God	(3 tapes)	$15.00
Forgiveness/Deliverance	(2 tapes)	$10.00
The Psalmist Ministry	(2 tapes)	$10.00
The Spirit of a Warrior	(2 tapes)	$10.00
Songs of The Lord	(1 tape)	$ 5.00
Hidden In God	(1 tape)	$ 5.00
Passion For God/Compassion For People	(1 tape)	$ 5.00
Songs of The Lord	(1 tape)	$ 5.00

BOOKS

The Costly Anointing	$9.00
The Requirements For Greatness	$9.00
A Wounded Spirit: It's Causes and Cures	$7.00

OR MAIL THIS FORM WITH YOUR CHECK, M.O OR C.C. INFO

Order Form

QTY	ITEM NAME	PRICE	TOTAL
	SUBTOTAL		
	10% Shipping/Handling		
	Love Gift		
	TOTAL ENCLOSED		

Method of Payment: ❏ Check   ❏ Money Order
                    ❏ VISA   ❏ Master Card

Card No: _____ Exp: _____ / _____

Signature: _____

Name _____

Address _____

City _____ ST _____ ZIP _____

Phone No. (_____) _____

Send orders and correspondance to: *Spirit to Spirit Ministry*
8200 W. County Line Rd. • Mequon, WI • 53097
Or Call: 1-414-238-1101 Fax: 1-414-238-1103